Pocket
TAIPEI

TOP SIGHTS · LOCAL LIFE · MADE EASY

Dinah Gardner

In This Book

QuickStart Guide

Your keys to understanding the city – we help you decide what to do and how to do it

Need to Know
Tips for a smooth trip

Neighbourhoods
What's where

Explore Taipei

The best things to see and do, neighbourhood by neighbourhood

Top Sights
Make the most of your visit

Local Life
The insider's city

The Best of Taipei

The city's highlights in handy lists to help you plan

Best Walks
See the city on foot

Taipei's Best...
The best experiences

Survival Guide

Tips and tricks for a seamless, hassle-free city experience

Getting Around
Travel like a local

Essential Information
Including where to stay

Our selection of the city's best places to eat, drink and experience:

◎ **Sights**

❌ **Eating**

🅟 **Drinking**

⭐ **Entertainment**

🔒 **Shopping**

These symbols give you the vital information for each listing:

☏ Telephone Numbers	👪 Family-Friendly
◷ Opening Hours	🐾 Pet-Friendly
Ⓟ Parking	⊡ Bus
Ⓝ Nonsmoking	🚢 Ferry
@ Internet Access	Ⓜ Metro
🛜 Wi-Fi Access	Ⓢ Subway
🌱 Vegetarian Selection	⊖ London Tube
🄴 English-Language Menu	🚃 Tram
	🚆 Train

Find each listing quickly on maps for each neighbourhood:

Bar Hemingway

16 Ⓜ Map p233, B2

Legend has it that Hem self, wielding a machine erate this timber-pan ered bar during showpiece is a en by Papa ar s.com; Hôtel Rit ◷6.30pm-2a

Lonely Planet's Taipei

Lonely Planet Pocket Guides are designed to get you straight to the heart of the city.

Inside you'll find all the must-see sights, plus tips to make your visit to each one really memorable. We've split the city into easy-to-navigate neighbourhoods and provided clear maps so you'll find your way around with ease. Our expert authors have searched out the best of the city: walks, food, nightlife and shopping, to name a few. Because you want to explore, our 'Local Life' pages will take you to some of the most exciting areas to experience the real Taipei.

And of course you'll find all the practical tips you need for a smooth trip: itineraries for short visits, how to get around, and how much to tip the guy who serves you a drink at the end of a long day's exploration.

It's your guarantee of a really great experience.

Our Promise

You can trust our travel information because Lonely Planet authors visit the places we write about, each and every edition. We never accept freebies for positive coverage, so you can rely on us to tell it like it is.

QuickStart Guide 7

Explore Taipei 21

Worth a Trip:

The Best of Taipei 127

Taipei's Best Walks

Taipei's Best ...

Survival Guide 145

QuickStart Guide

Welcome to Taipei

Taipei is the Yin and Yang of cities: modern malls and trading towers stack next to smoky temples and Qing era shophouses. Its beauty is born from a blend of Chinese, Japanese, Southeast Asian and American influences, seen from its cuisine to the courtesy of its people. Taipei today is a celebration of tolerance and taste. Welcome to Asia's most progressive capital!

Taipei skyline, dominated by Taipei 101 (p100)
TRISTAN TAN / SHUTTERSTOCK©

Taipei
Top Sights

Taipei 101 (p100)

This slimline symbol of the city stands head and shoulders above everything else. Get your eagle-eyed cityscape view from the observation deck in the clouds.

JACK HONG / SHUTTERSTOCK ©

National Palace Museum (p114)

World-class and absorbing collection of Chinese antiquities, rich in history,
exquisite in entirety. No excuses, you must visit.

Chiang Kai-shek Memorial Hall (p24)

This massive public square takes one's breath away in sheer scale of space and the grandeur of the neoclassical structures. Don't miss the slick quick changing of the guards.

Bao'an Temple (p42)

Gorgeously decorated and lovingly restored, these shadow-filled halls of folk religious worship promise magic from a bygone age.

Dihua Street (p44)

The many crumbling and renovated shophouses and mansions of this old tea-trading port have been carefully renovated into lovely cafes, restaurants and shops without losing the messy market vibe of its past.

Shilin Night Market
(p116)

Taipei's biggest, boldest night market remains a firm favourite. Fill up on all the sweet, savoury and sticky delights, and then wind your way through the maze to the Taoist temple at its centre.

Maokong Gondola
(p84)

Ride monkey-like over the treetops to Taipei's tea mountain on this exhilarating 30-minute glide in a glass-bottomed cable car.

Huashan 1914 Creative Park (p26)

Like a playpen for art-curious adults, this converted factory complex from the Japanese era pleases with heritage architecture, fun exhibitions, live music, designer spaces and classy eats.

Taipei Local Life

Insider tips to help you find the real city

Taipei's tourist sights are world class, but what makes a trip here so special is sensing the city's true vibe, looking beneath the surface to see what makes it tick.

A Saunter Around Songshan (p88)

▶ Night markets of snacks and shoes
▶ Lover's point, riverside

Come evening, Songshan emerges as a centre for consuming goods of all kinds from pork buns to spangly bras. Dragon-guarded temples remind us to pay our respects between purchases. The river offers an escape from the crowds, chatter and bargaining, and a place where young couples seal their bond.

Dining & Drinking in Dongmen (p72)

▶ Crumbling prison walls
▶ Restaurants and bars

This is the eat, drink, and be merry – decorously – district. As dusk falls, office workers gather to drink a pint; families converge for chopstick-clattering dinners. This genteel neighbourhood also harbours quiet points of reflection, remnants of Japanese rule and memories of controversial leaders.

Shopping in Xinyi (p102)

▶ Ritzy shopping malls
▶ Tai chi in the park

On weekends, Xinyi explodes with shoppers – happy snacking, relaxing with tea, and stopping to listen to street singers. This is modern Taipei, international Taipei, looking forward to a better future. In contrast, on the western fringe is the shady wooded Zhongshan Park where the retired carve out a little mellow corner.

Riding up the River (p124)

▶ Flea market
▶ Bird nature park

On weekends and holidays, the riverside paths become winding lanes of cyclists, joggers and friends just out for a stroll or walking their dog. At one point all is peace – the city skyline reflecting in the water, forests of reeds, dotted with water birds and turtles – the next erupts in a carnival of families picnicking and playing sports.

Xinyi (p98)

Cyclists on Taipei's riverside path (p124)

Other great places to experience the city like a local:

Pablo (p34)

Miramar Entertainment Park (p56)

Tianhou Temple (p65)

Chi Fan Shi Tang (p78)

1001 Nights Hookah Lounge Bar (p95)

Village 44 (p106)

Cafe Dogs & Cats (p122)

Taipei
Day Planner

Day One

Rocket straight up to the observation deck of **Taipei 101** (p100) for a bird's-eye view of the city. Imagine your next four days. It's a short stroll via some of Xinyi's swanky shopping malls to **Sun Yat-sen Memorial Hall** (p105) where on the hour you can watch the changing of the guards. Double back south to **Village 44** (p105) and explore these restored homes for Chinese soldiers.

After lunch at **Good Cho's** (p107), grab a YouBike and pedal west to **Da'an Forest Park** (p76) to enjoy its leafy landscape and ponds of sunbathing turtles. Wheel past **Taipei Grand Mosque** (p76) – if it's Friday prayers you might catch the city's Indonesian workers going to worship. Leave your bike at Dongmen MRT and slip into a time capsule of nostalgia at **Formosa Vintage Museum Cafe** (p76).

Queue up for Dinner at **Yongkang Beef Noodles** (p77) then, after dining, enjoy a secret cocktail at **Ounce Taipei** (p80) or tea at **Wistaria** (p80), or shop for bargains and late-night snacks at **Tonghua Night Market** (p82).

Day Two

Admire the devotional atmosphere at one of Taipei's oldest temples, **Longshan** (p63). Shake a couple of moon blocks to divine your future. When you're ready, head out and grab a crisp chilled cup of roselle tea from **Herb Alley** (p67) and then explore the Qing- and Japanese-era historic lane of **Bopiliao** (p65), which is now home to ad hoc art galleries. Wind your way north to the youth shopping district of Ximen, by which time you will probably be hungry.

Lunch at **Zhen Siwei** (p65), then continue today's history theme by catching a cab to the old Japanese quarter. Take photos of the old beautifully preserved shopfronts in **Dihua Street** (p125) and play with the myriad of fabrics – you could even get something made by the tailors on-site – at **Yongle Market** (p58). Nip up to Taipei's oldest tea merchants, **Lin Hua Tai Tea Company** (p58), for some of their very best white-tip oolong.

Make reservations for dinner at **Qing Tian Xia** (p51). After, catch a late showing of an indie film at **SPOT – Taipei Film House** (p57) or stay on Dihua St for a nightcap at **Le Zinc** (p56).

Short on time?
We've arranged Taipei's must-sees into these day-by-day itineraries to make sure you see the very best of the city in the time you have available.

Day Three

Head to **Bao'an Temple** (p42) early in the morning, before the crowds, and enjoy the temple at its most peaceful. Nip across the road to the **Confucius Temple** (p48) and get a primer on Confucian thought with some excellent hands-on exhibits. Heading back to the MRT you'll find **Taipei Expo Park** (p49). The best way to cover a lot of ground is to hop on a YouBike again. Take your pick of sights here; by far the best is the **Lin Antai Historic House** (p50).

Go Japanese for lunch at **Addiction Aquatic Development** (p52). Cross the river, admiring the self-conscious grandeur of the **Grand Hotel** (on top of Jiantan Hill) and take a stroll around the Generalissimo's country manor at the **Shilin Official Residence** (p119). Hop on a bus to the **National Palace Museum** (p114); towards the evening crowds thin considerably. If you've got time, cross the road to take in the excellent **Shung Ye Museum of Formosan Aborigines** (p119). Make sure you hit the basement where there's a small display on headhunting and shamanism.

Grab dinner at **Shilin Night Market** (p116) or head to **Din Tai Fung** (p121). In the evening, opt for sultry jazz at **Brown Sugar Live & Restaurant** (p110) or club till dawn at **Myst** (p109).

Day Four

Start with a free tour (book beforehand) of the **Presidential Office Building** (p30). Note the guards in the courtyard. Stroll around the government buildings in this district – many are fine examples of colonial architecture. Grab a cup of refreshing sour plum juice from **Lao Pai Gongyuan Hao** (p37) and enjoy it in the mellow greenery of **2-28 Peace Memorial Park** (p130), dedicated to those who died in the 2-28 Incident.

Eat at **Tim Ho Wan** (p34); if you don't want to wait, dine at **Auntie Xie's** (p34). Avoid the impossible labyrinth that is Taipei Main Station and instead head over to **Chiang Kai-shek Memorial Hall** (p24) to muse on the man responsible for Taiwan's White Terror. Pop into the **National Theatre & Concert Hall** (p37) to buy a ticket for tonight's show. Celebrate with the city's finest example of Taiwanese bubble tea at **Chun Shui Tang** (p36). As dusk approaches grab a cab to **Treasure Hill** (p31), the old artist colony on the riverbank. Remember to wear mosquito repellent.

Have dinner at **Madame Jill's Vietnamese Cuisine** (p34). After the show head over for a beer or wine in **Costumice's garden** (p80). If you've still got some energy, check out Taipei's famous 24-hour bookshop, in **Eslite** (p83).

Need to Know

**For more information,
see Survival Guide (p145)**

Currency
New Taiwanese Dollar (NT$)

Languages
Mandarin, Taiwanese and English

Visas
Tourists from most European countries, Canada, the US, Australia (see Taiwan's Ministry of Foreign Affairs website for updates), New Zealand, South Korea and Japan are given visa-free entry for stays of up to 90 days.

Money
ATMs are widely available; credit cards are accepted at most midrange and top-end hotels and at top-end restaurants.

Mobile Phones
Most foreign mobile phones can use local SIM cards with prepaid plans, which you can purchase at airport arrival terminals and top up at telecom outlets or convenience stores.

Time
National Standard Time (GMT/UTC plus eight hours)

Tipping
Tipping is not customary in restaurants or taxis (but is still appreciated). Midrange restaurants and above usually add a 10% service charge.

① Before You Go

Your Daily Budget

Budget: Less than NT$3000
▶ Dorm bed: NT$400–800
▶ Noodles or rice dish: NT$80–150
▶ Public transport: NT$80–150

Midrange: NT$3000–8000
▶ Double room in a hotel: NT$2500–4000
▶ Two-course dinner with wine: NT$800–1000
▶ Public transport and two short taxi trips: NT$400

Top end: More than NT$8000
▶ Double room in a top-end hotel: NT$6000–12,000
▶ Dinner at a fancy restaurant: NT$2000
▶ Theatre ticket: NT$1500

Useful Websites

Lonely Planet (www.lonelyplanet.com/taiwan/taipei) Destination low-down, hotel bookings.

Travel.Taipei (www.taipeitravel.net/en) Taipei city government's tourist guide to the capital.

Taipei MRT (english.trtc.com.tw) Maps the city and gives travel advice.

Advance Planning

▶ Check your passport is valid for at least six months (US for duration of stay; Japan three months).

▶ Inform your debit-/credit-card company you're heading away.

▶ Bring two pieces of identification – it will make it easier to buy a local SIM card.

② Arriving in Taipei

✈ From Taiwan Taoyuan International Airport

Getting into town from this airport is easy if a little time-consuming – usually between 45 to 90 minutes. There are taxis, a fleet of buses and a bus–high speed rail combination all going to central Taipei. An MRT line between Taipei Main Station and the airport was being constructed at the time of writing. It should be open in the first half of 2017. As a rough guide, the airport to downtown Taipei taxi fare will be around NT$1200, the bus–high speed rail combination will cost NT$190, while the airport buses average around NT$125.

✈ From Taipei Songshan Airport

If you arrive here, you are already in the city. There's an MRT station and taxis wait directly outside.

🚉 From Tapei Main Station

The terminal for most Taipei-bound trains is in the centre of the city and serviced by two MRT lines, taxis and buses.

③ Getting Around

Public transport is safe, efficient, clean and easy to use. It's also inexpensive. Buy an EasyCard in MRT stations (NT$100 return-able deposit). They can be topped up at MRT stations and convenience stores and used on the MRT, buses, some train services including high speed rail, for YouBike hire, and to buy goods in many high-street shops and food outlets. Alternatively, the Taipei-Pass gives unlimited travel (NT$180 for one day to NT$700 for five days) on MRT and buses. Buy them at MRT stations.

Ⓜ MRT

The quickest way to get around is the MRT; it has five colour-coded lines and is super reliable. Trains run from 6am to midnight.

🚲 Bicycle

Hire YouBikes for the city; mountain bikes for trails. Most MRT stations and tourist sights have YouBike stations.

🚗 Taxi

Yellow cabs are reasonably priced and ubiquitous, but traffic can be frustrating. Most drivers won't speak English, so make sure your destination is written down in Chinese. Short journeys in the city will average NT$300.

🚌 Bus

For visitors, buses are not as useful as MRT because routes are in Chinese only and they often get stuck in traffic, but it's a good network. Buses run approximately between 5am to 11pm.

Walking

If you stick to one or two neighbouring districts, Taipei is a very walkable city.

Taipei Neighbourhoods

Zhongshan & Datong (p40)

The historical quarter, with restored temple complexes, puppet theatres, and Qing-era shopfronts mixed with cafes and wine bars.

⊙ Top Sights

Bao'an Temple

Dihua Street

Ximending & Wanhua (p60)

Gritty, messy and true to life. Traditional temples thronging with prayer, dubious backstreets and a neon-bathed youth shopping hub.

Zhongzheng (p22)

The capital's political heart. Admire colonial grandeur, tree-lined boulevards, memorial parks, halls and museums.

⊙ Top Sights

Chiang Kai-shek Memorial Hall

Huashan 1914 Creative Park

Shilin Night Market
⊙

⊙
Bao'an Temple

⊙ **Dihua Street**

Huashan 1914
Creative Park

⊙
Chiang Kai-shek Memorial Hall

National
Palace ⊙
Museum

Shilin (p112)
Gateway to the hills' fresh air, ancient treasures in a world-class setting, the changing of the guard and a brilliant night-market.

⊙ Top Sights
National Palace Museum

Shilin Night Market

Worth a Trip
⊙ Top Sight
Maokong Gondola (p84)

Songshan (p86)
Sprawling with rowdy night-time markets, the Las Vegas of temples, and a sleepy, funky neighbourhood of hip local designers.

Xinyi (p98)
This is Taipei's top real estate, planted with glassed towers and malls. Dig deeper to find heritage sites, parks and a mountain trail.

⊙ Top Sight
Taipei 101

Taipei
101
⊙

Da'an (p70)
Modern and middle-class, a university district meets high-street shopping, boutiques, cafes and cosmopolitan restaurants.

Explore
Taipei

Worth a Trip

Raohe Street Night Market (p92)
R.NAGY / SHUTTERSTOCK ©

Explore

Zhongzheng

Named after Taiwan's first President Chiang Kai-shek (whose preferred given name was Chiang Chung-cheng), this central district includes most of the government offices as well as museums, memorial parks, historical sites and the capital's transport hub, Taipei Main Station. This is where you'll get a taste of Taiwan's recent history and a sense of its political struggles.

The Sights in a Day

Start the morning with a tour of the **Presidential Office Building** (p30). Break for a coffee with the dinosaurs in the **Land Bank Exhibition Hall** (p30) followed by a sobering walk through the **2-28 Memorial Museum** (p30). For lunch, opt for a bit of Michelin-star magic at **Tim Ho Wan** (p34)'s.

Digest that dim sum with a constitutional stroll around the **Botanical Gardens** (p31; pictured left) or a riverside walk or cycle in Gongguan. While you're here, check out the alternative artist enclave of **Treasure Hill** (p31). Feeling peckish? Queue up at **Lan Jia** (p32) for some classic pork-bun action.

Opt for Southeast Asian, with dinner at **Madame Jill's Vietnamese Cuisine** (p34), then it's time for a night at the opera. Enjoy a pre-dinner show at the **National Theatre & Concert Hall** (p37), stopping to admire the hushed grandeur of **Chiang Kai-shek Memorial** (p24) and Liberty Sq all lit up by lamps.

 Top Sights

Chiang Kai-shek Memorial Hall (p24)

Huashan 1914 Creative Park (p26)

Best of Taipei

Best Dining
Fuhang Soy Milk (p34)

Best Shopping
National Cultural & Creative Gift Centre (p38)

Huashan 1914 Creative Park (p26)

Best Bars
Revolver (p37)

Getting There

Ⓜ **MRT** The intersection of the red and blue lines at Taipei Main Station is the hub which will take you to all of the places in Zhongzheng. The main stations are Taipei Main, NTU Hospital and Chiang Kai-shek Memorial.

Top Sights
Chiang Kai-shek Memorial Hall

Taipei's vast public square is an imposing sight, flanked on three sides by neoclassical structures – Chiang Kai-shek's memorial with its white, white walls and blue roof in front and the National Theatre and Concert Hall (p37) on either side. It's certainly a must-see for all visitors to Taiwan, not only for the spectacle itself but because it opens a window onto the complicated political history of Taiwan.

中正紀念堂; Zhōngzhèng Jìniàn Táng

👁 Map p28, C3

www.cksmh.gov.tw

21 Zhongshan S Rd; 中山南路21號

🕑9am-6pm

Ⓜ Chiang Kai-shek Memorial Hall

From Autocracy to Liberty

This grandiose monument to authoritarian leader Chiang Kai-shek is a popular attraction and rightly so. It is a sobering feeling standing in the massive courtyard. Chiang's blue-roofed hall is a prime example of the neoclassical style, favoured as a counterpoint to the Cultural Revolution's rejection of classical culture in China.

In 2007 the surrounding park was renamed Liberty Square in honour of Taiwan's long road to democracy – many pro-democracy protests in the 1980s took place here.

Chiang for the Chop?

With a new Democratic Progressive Party (DPP) government in power from 2016, the old debate of what to do with the memorial has resurfaced. Many people believe that honouring a man responsible for the White Terror is morally wrong. The latest idea has been to convert the sight into an archive for all Taiwanese presidents instead and use the space to commemorate protest movements in Taiwan.

Visiting

As you enter by the main gate, the symmetry of the three-hall arrangement is arresting. You can even see the silhouette of Chiang's statue in the shadow of his white monument in the distance. Everything about this square says power.

Entrance to the main hall is via a series of 89 steps (the age of Chiang when he died). Inside is an artefact museum with some Chiang memorabilia. The hourly changing of the honour guard is very popular.

You can comfortably explore the square in about an hour. Sitting atop its own MRT station, it makes a good first stop; from here there are many other tourist sights within walking distance.

BAI XIN / SHUTTERSTOCK ©

☑ Top Tips

▶ Admission is free.

▶ Every August or September the National Theatre & Concert Hall (p37) holds its Summer Jazz Outdoor Party: several evenings of free live jazz shows in the square.

▶ There are other occasional free outdoor performances throughout the year, and sometimes when big-name shows are sold out a large screen will be set up in the square for the public to watch. Ask at the Concert Hall for details.

▶ Note the colour of the guards' uniforms, they change every three months: blue is the air force, green is the land army and white is the navy.

✗ Take a Break

Enjoy a refreshing classic bubble tea and a bowl of noodles at Chun Shui Tang (p36) in the National Concert Hall.

Time for a beer? Head to Revolver (p37) for a pint of Red Point.

Top Sights
Huashan 1914 Creative Park

This warren of shops, cafes, boutiques and exhibition spaces, set in pleasant leafy grounds, has an arty rawness that attracts young hipsters as well as families and young couples. The complex is a refurbished wine and camphor factory zone dating back to the Japanese era. Now it's a great place to see the designs of Taiwan's young creative community in restored buildings from the distant past.

華山1914; Huàshān Yījiǔyīsì

⊙ Map p28, D1

www.huashan1914.com

admission free

Ⓜ Zhongxiao Xinsheng

Singer and actress Gui Gui at the *Case Closed* exhibition at Huashan 1914 Creative Park

From Wine to Sublime

The Japanese opened a factory here in 1916 as a private wine-making facility. When the Nationalists took over the factory once Japan lost WWII, they started using it to make cheap sweet potato wine.

It was finally shuttered in 1987 and the area would likely be just another block of overpriced city apartments today if not for arts groups who discovered, in 1997, that the old factory provided a perfect venue for performances, workshops and installations.

Rock & stroll

Huashan has a very energetic vibe, and this is reflected in how often many of the restaurants and all of the exhibitions change.

The main strip of grey factory buildings can be quite hectic because this is where Legacy Taipei (a music venue usually throbbing with indie and rock bands) and most of the exhibition spaces are located. Over at Huashan Brick Lane, on the other side of the chimney, things are more peaceful and the structures are handsome red-brick buildings.

Visiting

You could happily pass two or three hours here, including lunch, exploring the old buildings and browsing the pop-up shops. The factory grounds arc open 24/7, but hours for individual shops, restaurants and performance venues vary. There's an information centre near the front as you face the grounds off Bade Rd.

VCG / GETTY IMAGES ©

☑ Top Tips

▶ Start by popping into the information kiosk and getting an English map of the park; it explains what every building used to be.

▶ You can buy tickets for events around town at the information kiosk in the front of the park.

▶ Most Friday nights around 8pm a dance band called Swing meets to hold public dances in one of the park's open spaces.

✖ Take a Break

The park can get busy, so nip across the road to ROLA i COFFEE (p35) for a rich brew and a slice of creatively flavoured toast.

Here at night-time? Grab a table on Alleycat's (p35) outdoor deck and enjoy pizza and wine.

Da'an Forest Park

Xinsheng S Rd

Civic Blvd

Songjiang Rd

Bade Rd

Zhongxiao Xinsheng

Xinsheng S Rd

Xinyi Rd

Qingtian St

Yongkang St

Yongkang Park

Jinshan S Rd

Jinshan S Rd

Huashan 1914 Creative Park

Lishui St

Dongmen

29 16

Jinhua St

Jinhua Elementary School

Zhongxiao E Rd Section 4

Beiping E Rd

15

28 13 19

Qingdao E Rd

Shaoxing S Rd

Renai Rd

Xinyi Rd

Aiguo E Rd

Jinhua St

Linsen N Rd

Xuzhou Rd

18

Hangzhou S Rd

Tianjin St

Shandao Temple

Linsen S Rd

Zhenjiang Rd

Renai Rd

Chiang Kai-shek Memorial Hall

Xinyi Rd

17

Roosevelt Rd

Zhongshan S Rd

26

ZHONGZHENG

2-28 Memorial Museum

East Gate

Zhongshan S Rd

23

24

Taipei Main Station

Taipei Visitor Information Centre

Zhongxiao W Rd

12

Gongyuan Rd

Nanyang Rd

Guanqian St

Hualing St

2

NTU Hospital

Land Bank Exhibition Hall

Changde St

2-28 Memorial Peace Park

Ketagalan Blvd

Guiyang St

National Central Library

Aiguo W Rd

Chiang Kai-shek Memorial Hall

National Taiwan Craft Research & Development Institute

Nanhai Rd

National 2-28 Memorial Museum

Chongqing S Rd

Xiangyang Rd

1 20

Changsha St

Presidential Office Building

Chongqing S Rd

Bo'ai Rd

Aiguo W Rd

Xiaonanmen

4

8

Kaifeng St

Hankou St

Wuchang St

11

Hengyang Rd

Baoqing Rd

1

Botanical Gardens

6

National Museum of History

7

Yanping S Rd

Zhonghua Rd

DA'AN

Heping E Rd

Chaozhou St

Lishui St

Jinshan S Rd

Roosevelt Rd

Guting Ⓜ 22 ⊗ 10

Nanchang Rd

Jinjiang Rd

Tongan St

Heping W Rd

Tingzhou Rd

Guling St

Heping W Rd

Ningbo W Rd

Sanyuan St

Ningbo W St

Quanzhou St

Zhonghua Rd

Chongqing S Rd

Chongqing S Rd

Wenzhou St

Xinhai Rd

Longquan St

Lane 243 (Cafe Lane)

Shida Night Market

Shida Rd

Pucheng St

Lane 105

Lane 101

Roosevelt Rd

Shida Rd

National Taiwan Normal University (Shida)

Shuiyuan Rd

Shuiyuan Rd

Shuiyuan Rd

Pedestrian/ Bike Bridge

Xindian River

Xinsheng S Rd

Wenzhou St

Lane 86

Lane 283

Roosevelt Rd 27 Ⓜ Lane 240

21 Ⓜ Lane 210

Taipower Building Ⓜ

National Taiwan University

Lane 316 14 ⊗ Lane 24

Gongguan Ⓜ 25 ✿

Siyuan St

5 ▲

For reviews see

◉	Top Sights	p24
◉	Sights	p30
⊗	Eating	p32
◉	Drinking	p36
✿	Entertainment	p37
⬛	Shopping	p38

500 m

0.25 miles

N

Sights

Presidential Office Building

HISTORIC BUILDING

1 Map p28, A2

Built in 1919 as the seat of the Japanese governor general of Taiwan, this striking building has housed the offices of the Republic of China (ROC) president since 1949. Its classical European-fusion style includes many Japanese cultural elements, such as a sunrise-facing front, and a shape in the form of the character 日, part of 日本 (Japan), as seen from the air. All visitors need to book online three days before their visit. (總統府, Zǒngtǒng Fǔ; www.president.gov.tw; 122 Chongqing S Rd, Sec 1; 重慶南路一段122號; with passport free; ⊙9-11.30am Mon-Fri; Ⓜ NTU Hospital)

Land Bank Exhibition Hall

MUSEUM

2 Map p28, B1

Evolution is the theme at this museum, set in a 1930s former bank: evolution of life, evolution of money and banking, and evolution of the bank from the Japanese colonial era to modern Taipei. It's an odd juxtaposition but the displays at each level, from soaring sauropod fossils to the open bank vault, are well presented and rich in details. Tickets include admission to the **National Taiwan Museum**, located within the 2-28 park (p130). (土銀分館; Tǔyín Fēnguǎn;

02-2314 2699; www.ntm.gov.tw; 25 Xiangyang Rd; 襄陽路25號; NT$30; ⊙9.30am-5pm Tue-Sun; Ⓜ NTU Hospital)

2-28 Memorial Museum

MUSEUM

3 Map p28, B2

Located inside the 2-28 park (p130), the 2-28 Memorial Museum offers an explanation of the deaths that took place on 28 February 1947 and the repercussions that followed. Acknowledgement of the 2-28 Incident was a pivotal part of Taiwan's transformation from dictatorship to democracy. (二二八紀念館; Èr'èrbā Jìniànguǎn; 3 Ketagalan Blvd; 凱達格蘭大道3號; Mon-Fri NT$20, Sat-Sun free; ⊙10am-5pm Tue-Sun; Ⓜ NTU Hospital)

National 2-28 Memorial Museum

MUSEUM

4 Map p28, B4

This graceful memorial to the victims of the 2-28 Incident was opened in 2011. Housed in a beautiful Japanese building dating back to 1931, the permanent exhibition charts the tragic events of February 1947 and also includes a permanent exhibition calling for the establishment of a Truth and Reconciliation Committee to find those guilty. There is only occasional English-language signage, but multilingual audio guides are available. (二二國家紀念館; Èr'èr Guójiā Jìniànguǎn; http://museum.228.org.tw; 54 Nanhai Rd; 南海路54號; admission free; ⊙10am-5pm Tue-Sun; Ⓜ Chiang Kai-shek Memorial Hall)

TOPIMAGES / SHUTTERSTOCK ©

Treasure Hill

Treasure Hill
VILLAGE

5 Map p28, E8

Head down to the river from the **Museum of Drinking Water** (自來水園區; Zìláishuǐ Yuán Qū; 1 Siyuan St; 思源街1號; MGongguan), turn left, and you'll soon come across this charming art village founded in the late 1940s by soldiers who fled to Taiwan with Chiang Kai-shek. While praised for its 'living memories' and off-the-grid community lifestyle (villagers 'borrowed' electricity, set up organic farms by the river, built homes out of discarded materials and recycled grey water), the village underwent a makeover in 2010 and is now largely an artist village. (寶藏巖; Bǎozàng Yán; admission free; MGongguan)

Botanical Gardens
GARDENS

6 Map p28, A4

An oasis in the city, this 8-hectare park has well-stocked greenhouses, literature- and Chinese-zodiac-themed gardens, a lotus pond and myriad lanes where you can lose yourself in quiet contemplation. The gardens were established by the Japanese in 1921 and are part of a larger neighbourhood that maintains an old Taipei feel. Within the park, look for the **Qing administrative office**, built in 1888, and a **herbarium** from 1924. (植物園; Zhíwùyuán; 53 Nanhai Rd; 南海路53號; admission free; ⏰4am-10pm; MXiaonanmen)

National Museum of History

MUSEUM

7 Map p28, A4

Established in 1955 with a collection from Henan province, this is one of Taipei's best museums of Chinese art. Exhibits are small and cover the range of dynasties, but most works are masterpieces. Even the entrance corridor boasts exquisite Buddhist sculpture, including a mesmerising nine-layer stone tower with the thousand Buddhas motif. It hails from the 5th century AD. (國立歷史博物館; Guólì Lìshǐ Bówùguǎn; 02-2361 0270; www.nmh. gov.tw; 49 Nanhai Rd; 南海路49號; NT$30; 10am-6pm Tue-Sun; Chiang Kai-shek Memorial Hall)

National Taiwan Craft Research & Development Institute

ARTS CENTRE

8 Map p28, A4

This striking red and white building, with its circular neoclassical Chinese-style roof, dates back to just 1956. It was recently converted into the Craft Research & Development Centre where the first two floors showcase Taiwanese-designed and -made gift products – everything from stationery to silverware – while the top floors are reserved for art, architecture and craft exhibitions and a rooftop organic food court. There are fantastic views from the roof, where you can also get up close to the fantastical glazed roof tiles. (02-2356 3880; www.ntcri.gov.tw;

41 Nanhai Rd; 南海路41號; admission free; 9.30am-5.30pm Tue-Sun; Chiang Kai-shek Memorial Hall)

Eating

Lan Jia

TAIWANESE $

9 Map p28, E8

Lan Jia is widely regarded as having the best *guā bāo* (刮包) in Taiwan. What's *guā bāo*? Think of a savoury slow-braised pork hamburger with pickled mustard and ground peanuts stuffed inside a steamed bun. Yep, delicious, and it's starting to take the West by storm, with shops and trucks offering it now in London, Berlin and across the US. (藍家; Lán Jiā; 02-2368 1165; 3, Alley 8, Lane 316, Roosevelt Rd, Sec 3; 羅斯福路三段316巷8弄3號; steamed buns NT$50; 11am-midnight Tue-Sun; Gongguan)

Ooh Cha Cha

VEGAN $$

10 Map p28, C5

The place to go if you need an injection of healthiness and quite possibly the best Western vegan food in town. This small funky cafe with glass walls offers scrumptious salads, brown rice bowls and burgers, as well as cakes and smoothies. Ingredients are varied and creative, ranging from roasted garlic hummus to lemon avocado to purple lime beet balls. (02-2367 7133; 207 Nanchang Rd, Sec 2; 南昌路二段207號; dishes NT$240-280; 10am-9pm Sun-Thu, to 8pm Fri & Sat; Guting)

Understand

The 2-28 Incident

Contraband Cigarettes

Zhongzheng District is home to two memorial museums and a memorial park to the 2-28 Incident. What was this event?

On 27 February 1947, agents from the Tobacco Monopoly Bureau in Taipei seized contraband cigarettes and money from a middle-aged widow and pistol-whipped her into unconsciousness. Angry crowds formed and attacked the officers, one of whom responded by shooting into the crowd, killing an innocent bystander.

Violence Erupts

The next morning businesses closed in protest, and crowds gathered outside the Taipei branch of the Monopoly Bureau, attacking employees and setting the offices on fire. This was followed by an afternoon protest outside the governor general's office. Here, security forces again fired into the crowds, killing a number of protesters. Violent protests now erupted all over Taiwan and for several days the island was in chaos.

Troops from the Mainland arrived on 8 March and, according to witnesses, began three days of killing civilians. This was followed in the coming weeks by the round-up and summary execution of protest leaders, intellectuals, high-school students and anyone else considered suspect by the government. An estimated 18,000 to 28,000 people were killed during this period. Taiwan lost nearly its entire native elite.

Lifting of Martial Law

Until the lifting of martial law in 1987, there was little open discussion of the event. In 1992 President Lee Teng-hui made a public apology to victims on behalf of the government. Three years later he declared 28 February (2-28) a public holiday, and created a memorial foundation to deal with compensation. Taipei Park was renamed 2-28 Peace Memorial Park, and a 2-28 Memorial Museum was opened in the former radio station that had been taken over following the initial February protests.

Auntie Xie's

TAIWANESE $$

11 Map p28, A1

This very traditional and simple basement restaurant is a secret favourite of locals. There's no menu: each diner chooses fish or meat and dishes are decided by the kitchen that day. Auntie Xie's signature dish is the taro congee (芋頭粥; *yùtou zhōu*). (謝阿姨; Xiè Āyí; ☑ 02-2388 1012; basement, 122 Bo'ai Rd; 博愛路122號B1; set menus NT$350; ⏱ 11.30am-2pm & 5.30-830pm; ❄; Ⓜ Ximen)

Tim Ho Wan

DIM SUM $$

12 Map p28, B1

There are always long queues outside this Hong Kong dim sum chain, likely generated by its one Michelin star and

the relatively low cost. To avoid a horrendous wait, come here on a weekday after 2pm. Try the spinach dumplings with shrimp – they are transparent. (添好運; Tiān Hǎoyùn; 36 Zhongxiao W Rd, Sec 1; 忠孝西路一段36號; dishes NT$98-138; ⏱ 10am-9.30pm; ❄; Ⓜ Taipei Main Station)

Fuhang Soy Milk

BREAKFAST $

13 Map p28, D1

A popular shop in the Huashan Market for a traditional Taiwanese breakfast such as *dòujiāng* (豆漿; soy milk), *yóutiáo* (油條; fried bread stick), *dàn bǐng* (蛋餅; spring onion–filled crepes and egg) and *shāobǐng* (燒餅; stuffed layered flat bread). Be prepared to wait – the queues of customers regularly snake down the stairs. Take exit 5 from Shandao Temple MRT station. (阜杭豆漿; Fùháng Dòujiāng; 2nd fl, Hushan Market, 108 Zhongxiao E Rd, Sec 1; 忠孝東路一段108號 華山市場; items NT$25-50; ⏱ 5.30am-12.30pm Tue-Sun; Ⓜ Shandao Temple)

Madame Jill's Vietnamese Cuisine

VIETNAMESE $$

14 Map p28, E8

Opened by Chinese fleeing the Vietnam War in 1974, Madame Jill's was Taipei's first Vietnamese restaurant and is still one of the best. Though there are a few sops to local tastes (such as the choice of Taiwanese or Vietnamese spring rolls), flavours are mostly authentic, and with a six-page menu there is plenty to choose from.

⦿ Local Life
Giant Tarts of Cheese

Pablo (B1, 36 Zhongxiao W Rd, Sec 1; 忠孝西路一段36號地下1樓; cakes NT$278-328; ⏱ 11am-10pm; ❄ ☑; Ⓜ Taipei Main Station) is the latest Japanese craze in Taipei. This little cafe in the basement, and its hole-in-the-wall takeway counter at street level, sell giant tarts of Japan's richer, gloopier take on cheesecake. The tarts can be happily shared between two or three people. As well as the best-selling original flavour there are cognac chocolate, berry and matcha varieties. Take exit M6 from Taipei Main Station.

National Taiwan Craft Research & Development Institute (p32)

(翠薪越南餐廳; Cuìxīn Yuènán Cāntīng; ☎02-2368 0254; 11, Lane 24, Roosevelt Rd, Sec 4; 羅斯福路四段24巷11號; dishes NT$120-220; ⏰11.20am-2.30pm & 5.20-9pm; ❄; Ⓜ Gongguan)

ROLA i COFFEE

CAFE $

15  Map p28, D1

Big doorstep slices of walnut bread topped with a range of sweet and savoury toppings are served here. Try the Chinese pear, berry and cream cheese or the asparagus and egg. The coffee here is also extremely good. (☎02-2321 6726; 28-1 Hangzhou N Rd; 杭州北路28−1號; toast NT$100-150; ⏰10.30am-6pm; ❄ 🛜; Ⓜ Zhongxiao Xinsheng)

Alleycat's

PIZZA $$

16  Map p28, E1

With its rustic-chic setting inside a former brick warehouse and perfected stone-oven recipes, this is one of the top spots for pizza in Taipei. You can sit indoors under a soaring vaulted ceiling, or outdoors in a garden zone. Calzoni, panini and appetisers are available, as is a good selection of beer on tap. Salads are poor value. (www.alleycatspizza.com; Huashan 1914 Culture Park; pizzas from NT$300; ⏰11am-11pm Sun-Thu, to 1am Fri & Sat; 🛜; Ⓜ Shandao Temple)

Drinking

Chun Shui Tang
TRADITIONAL DRINKS

17 🚇 Map p28, C3

The pearl milk tea here is supposed to be the best in the city – pink, frothy and creamy with smaller, firmer pearls and only lightly sweetened. There are branches of Chun Shui Tang across the city but this one, located on the ground floor of the National Concert Hall, is one of the nicest. Traditional light noodle dishes and Chinese desserts are also available. (春水堂; Chūnshuǐ Táng; www.chunshuitang. com.tw; ground fl, National Concert Hall; ⏰11.30am-8.30pm; Ⓜ Chiang Kai-shek Memorial Hall)

Mayor's Residence Art Salon
CAFE

18 🚇 Map p28, D2

Built in 1940, this is one of the best-preserved large Japanese-style residences in Taiwan. With its heritage styling, great natural lighting and garden, this is a superb place to grab a coffee, tea or light meal. Art exhibits are frequently held here. (市長官邸藝文沙龍; Shìzhǎng Guāndǐ Yìwén Shālóng; www.mayorsalon.tw; 46 Xuzhou Rd; 徐州路46號; ⏰9am-9pm; 📶; Ⓜ Shandao Temple)

Funky
GAY

19 🚇 Map p28, D1

In operation since 1991, this is still one of the most popular gay clubs in

---

Understand
LGBTIQ Taipei

Gay and lesbian travellers will find Taipei friendly and exciting. An open-minded city, Taipei hosts Asia's largest **Gay Pride parade** (台灣同志遊行; Táiwān Tóngzhì Yóuxíng; www.twpride.org; admission free; ⏰last Sat in Oct) every October. It's common to see LGBT couples holding hands on the streets, though not common to see them kissing. The centre of gay nightlife is the bar and restaurant area around the Red House (p64) in Ximending.

Useful resources include **Utopia** (www.utopia-asia.com), **Taiwan LGBT Hotline Association** (www.hotline.org.tw/english) and **Taiwan LGBT Pride** (www.twpride.org).

While in Taipei you can get up-to-date information on gay nightlife options from Toto at **three little birds** (美好日子; Měihǎo Rìzi; www.threelittlebirdstpe. com; 10, Lane 62, Taishun St, 泰順街62巷10號; dm/d from NT$550/NT$1700; ▣✳📶; Ⓜ Taipower Building) hostel. A community of lesbians often meets at Love Boat (p38); ask for Olivia.

Taipei, attracting both an international and a local crowd. Somewhere down in the basement there is karaoke. (B1-10, Hangzhou S Rd, Sec 1; 杭州南路一段10號B1; ⏱9.30pm-late; Ⓜ Shandao Temple)

Lao Pai Gongyuan Hao
TRADITIONAL DRINKS

20 Map p28, B2

Across from 2-28 park in an old Japanese-era corner shop is this decades-old place selling a refreshing *suān méitāng* (酸梅湯; sour plum juice). (老牌公園號; Lǎopái Gōngyuán Hào; ☎02-2311 3009; 2 Hengyang Rd; 衡陽路2號; drinks NT$25; ⏱10.30am-8pm; Ⓜ NTU Hospital)

H*ours Cafe
CAFE

21 Map p28, D7

Lovely little gay-owned cafe and bookshop serving simple snacks and beverages. (☎02-2364 2742; www.facebook.com/hours.cafe; 12, Alley 8, Lane 210, Roosevelt Rd, Sec 3; 羅斯福路三段210巷8弄12號; ⏱2-11pm; 🛜; Ⓜ Taipower Building)

Cafe Macho
CAFE

22 Map p28, C5

The name may be macho but the staff are typically super-smiley young Taiwanese women. Inside, the decor is industrial chic, with concrete flooring and brick walls. If you need a spell on your laptop, go for the long high table with power points.

At night the place turns into a bar, with a small smoking garden outside. But the best thing here is the Baileys latte. (早秋咖啡; Zǎoqiū Kāfēi; ☎02-2368 5029; www.facebook.com/CafeMacho; 10 Jinjiang St; 晉江街10號; ⏱noon-midnight; 🛜; Ⓜ Guting)

Entertainment

National Theatre & Concert Hall
CONCERT VENUE

23 Map p28, B3

Located inside Liberty Sq, the National Theatre & Concert Hall host large-scale concerts and cultural events including dances, musicals, Chinese and Western opera and concerts of Chinese and Western classical and popular music. The halls, completed in 1987, were among the first major performance venues built in Asia. The National Theatre was closed for refurbishment at the time of updating, and is due to reopen in February 2017. (國家戲劇院, 國家音樂廳; Guójiā Xìjù Yuàn, Guójiā Yīnyuè Tīng; ☎02-3393 9888; www.ntch.edu.tw; Liberty Sq; 🛜; Ⓜ Chiang Kai-shek Memorial Hall)

Revolver
LIVE MUSIC

24 Map p28, B3

Revolver is one of Taipei's liveliest spots for drinking and live music. It's also very popular with expats and foreign students who start spilling

Top Tip

Getting around

The lovely leafy boulevards in the area are perfect for cycling around as long as you avoid the snarl of roads around Taipei Main Station. The best places to set off with your YouBike are NTU Hospital MRT station or Gongguan MRT station, from where you can explore National Taiwan University or the riverside bike paths on your wheels.

out onto the street by 8pm. This bar/pub/dance club is a great place to catch a live music act, hang out, play pool and drink cheapish beer. (www.revolver.tw; 1 Roosevelt Rd, Sec 1; 羅斯福路一段; live music upstairs NT$300; ☾6.30pm-3am Mon-Sat, to 1am Sun; �︎; MChiang Kai-shek Memorial Hall)

Wall Live House
LIVE MUSIC

 25 ⭐ Map p28, E8

The cavernous Wall Live House is Taipei's premier venue for independent music, both local and international. Descend the dark stairs and smell the stale beer. This is very definitely the place for the cool indie kids. (www.thewall.com.tw; B1, 200 Roosevelt Rd, Sec 4; 羅斯福路四段200號B1; club NT$200, bands from NT$500; ☾8pm-late; MGongguan)

Shopping

National Cultural & Creative Gift Centre
GIFTS & SOUVENIRS

26 Map p28, C2

Four floors of jade, ceramics, tea sets, jewellery, scrolls, Kinmen knifes, Kavalan whisky and handmade soap are just highlights of the variety on offer here. Colourful Franz porcelain is featured in a special section. (國家文創禮品館; Guójiā Wénchuàng Lǐpǐn Guǎn; www.handicraft.org.tw; 1 Xuzhou Rd; 徐州路1號; ☾9am-6pm; �︎; MNTU Hospital)

Love Boat
ADULT

27 Map p28, E7

A shop for the lesbian community with both in-store and online sales. In recent years it's expanded into a cafe and hosts local events and tarot card readings. There's a good range of merchandise from sex toys to suits. (愛之船拉拉時尚概念館; Àizhī Chuán Lālā Shíshàng Gàiniàn Guǎn; www.lesloveboat. com; 11, Lane 240, Roosevelt Rd, Sec 3; 羅斯福路三段240巷11號; ☾2-10pm Tue-Sun; MTaipower Building)

Aboriginal Artworks
ARTS & CRAFTS

28 Map p28, D1

On the ground floor of compact Huashan Market this little stall sells some curious indigenous handicrafts, brightly coloured with bold geometric designs. Highlights include bottles of

National Theatre & Concert Hall (p37)

potent sweet rice wine, hand-sewn phone cases and unusual table lamps. (Hushan Market, 108 Zhongxiao E Rd, Sec1; 華山市場忠孝東路一段108號; ⏰9am-7pm Tue-Sun; Ⓜ Shandao Temple)

VVG Thinking
GIFTS & SOUVENIRS

29 🔒 Map p28, D1

Located in the funky loft space above a fusion restaurant in the Huashan 1914 Creative Park (p26) is this quirky, boutique book and design shop with a rich collection of art books and cookbooks, vintage collectables and designer products. VVG is in the complex of red-brick buildings to the west of the giant smokestack. (好樣思維; Hǎo Yàng Sīwéi; Huashan 1914 Creative Park; ⏰noon-9pm; Ⓜ Zhongxiao Xinsheng)

Explore

Zhongshan & Datong

Datong (大同; Dàtóng; Dadaocheng) is one of the oldest areas of the city. There's a new vibe to the Dihua St area, which still retains its Qing- and Japanese-era mansions and shops, and don't miss the temples in this district. Zhongshan (中山; Zhōngshān) was once a centre for finance and international business and today it is still loaded with hotels and almost endless eateries (especially Japanese).

The Sights in a Day

☀ Take advantage of the early morning hush to watch the faithful pray at **Bao'an Temple** (p42). The **Confucius Temple** (p48) is just next door so budget another 30 minutes or so for some philosophical pondering among the interactive displays. When it's time for a break, there's coffee and fresh juice in Maji Square inside **Taipei Expo Park** (p49).

☼ On the other side of the park is the ever popular **Addiction Aquatic Development** (p52), where you can pick up a fresh sushi lunch at this lively Japanese food market before heading back west to the old-world charm of **Dihua Street** (p44). The old shop fronts and ivy-covered brickwork are a photographer's delight.

☾ As evening draws on, walk across to **Ningxia Night Market** (p52) for some laid-back snacking or stay in Dihua St for fine dining at **Qing Tian Xia** (p51). Catch an arthouse film at **SPOT** (p57) or go local with a night at the traditional opera – try **Taipei Eye** (p58) or **Dadaocheng Theatre** (p57).

 Top Sights

Bao'an Temple (p42)

Dihua Street (p44)

💗 **Best of Taipei**

Dining

Qing Tian Xia (p51)

Addiction Aquatic Development (p52)

Goose & Seafood (p52)

RAW (p52)

Entertainment

Taiyuan Asian Puppet Theatre Museum (p56)

SPOT – Taipei Film House (p57)

Taipei Eye (p58)

Getting There

Ⓜ **MRT** The green (between Beiman and Nanjing Fuxing), red (between Zhongshan and Yuanshan) and orange (between Daqiaotou and Xingtian Temple) lines cover most of Zhongshan and Datong. The two key stations are Zhongshan and Yuanshan.

Top Sights
Bao'an Temple

Rich in history, deep in devotion, Bao'an Temple is a magnificent and elaborately decorated complex of 18th-century worship halls. Taipei has hundreds of temples, but Bao'an is the real historic deal. Its modern restoration was so painstakingly done it won a Unesco award.

保安宮; Bǎoān Gōng

◉ Map p46, B2

www.baoan.org.tw/
english

61 Hami St; 哈密街61號

admission free

⊙7am-10pm

Ⓜ Yuanshan

Don't Miss

Free Festivities

Following a massive renovation project using skilled artisans and top-quality materials, the temple began holding an annual folk-arts festival (called **Baosheng Cultural Festival**) from March to June, which includes the Five Day Completion Rituals to Thank Gods (essentially to transform the temple from an everyday to a sacred space), the gods' birthday celebrations, lion dances, parades, Taiwanese opera performances and even free Chinese medicine clinics. See the temple's website or the Taipei City Government's website (www.taipei.gov.tw) for dates of events, all of which are free.

God of Medicine

Bao'an's main deity is Emperor Baosheng (or Wu) who studied Chinese medicine and became a great healer, although he himself died at the age of 58. He didn't treat just humans; legend has it that he cured a dragon of a painful eye and removed a hairpin from the throat of a tiger. He is revered as a god of medicine and people come here to ask him for good health.

A Bemused Octopus

This truly beautiful folk-religion temple deserves a slow, thoughtful exploration. Bao'an is a kaleidoscope of deep rich browns, reds and blacks, and the carvings and paintwork are noticeably more elaborate than usual. There are countless small room shrines along both sides. Of particular note are the roof trusses, the ceramic dragons, the small exorcism room at the back, and the painting on the back wall – notice the fish-headed warrior and the bemused octopus.

☑ Top Tips

▶ Come in the early morning before the tour groups; this is when locals come for quiet prayer.

▶ If you're here between March and June, try to attend one of the parades or rituals in the temple's annual folk-arts festival.

▶ There's an information office with a brochure on Bao'an at the rear right of the temple's inner courtyard.

✗ Take a Break

Pop over the road to the small coffee and tea shop in the Confucius Temple (p48). It serves hot and cold drinks as well as creatively flavoured homemade ice lollies – lavender, cherry-rose and Earl Grey, among others.

The Maji Square (Maji Maji) outdoor food court at Taipei Expo Park (p49) is great for inexpensive Western, Indian, Taiwanese and Thai.

Top Sights
Dihua Street

The most atmospheric of all Taipei's districts, Dihua St is a must-see for anyone interested in architecture and history. The many crumbling and renovated shophouses and mansions of this old tea-trading port are excellent examples of old Fujianese, Western colonial, and baroque (from the Japanese influence) architecture. Many of the renovated premises are now lovely cafes, restaurants and shops, but the area still retains the messy echoes of the past.

迪化街; Díhuà Jiē

◉ Map p46, A8

Ⓜ Zhongshan, Daqiaotou

Don't Miss

From Tea to Tourism

The street was constructed in the 1850s after merchants on the losing side of an ethnic feud in the Wanhua area fled to Dadaocheng. After Taiwan's ports were opened following the Second Opium War (1856–60), Western tea merchants flooded into the area and built handsome mansions and trading stores. Later, during the Japanese era, baroque and modernist architectural and decorative touches were added to many shops, making Dihua Taipei's most historically diverse street.

The Flashpoint of the 28 February Incident

If you walk up Nanjing W Rd for about five minutes you will come to a stone plaque that marks the spot that sparked the 28 February Incident (p33). This is where on 27 February 1947, police beat an impoverished cigarette vendor for selling contraband, sparking an uprising and subsequent bloody crackdown.

Visiting

The first house/shop on the street is at 156 Dihua St, Sec 1. Notice its low profile and narrow arcades. Further up the street, near Minquan W Rd, are typical shops from the late 19th century with arched windows and wide arcades. Closer to Yongle Market are the Western-style merchant houses and shops renovated during Japanese times.

The closest MRT stations are Beimen and Zhongshan, from where it's a five- to 10-minute walk. A more fun way is by bike along the riverside paths. Exit the path from Dadaocheng Wharf, which is just two blocks away.

☑ **Top Tips**

▶ The lower stretch of Dihua St can get a bit touristy; to escape the crowds head to the upper part (north of Guisui St) or just explore the surrounding lanes.

▶ There are lots of surprises. Stop off at the in Blooom (p58) shop and pick up a very good hand-drawn map of the area.

✕ **Take a Break**

For quiche and coffee in a delectable courtyard, pop into Salt Peanuts (p53).

When it's time for dinner, reserve a table at Qing Tian Xia (p51).

SHILIN

DATONG

ZHONGSHAN

Keelung River

Dajia Riverside Park

National Revolutionary Martyrs' Shrine

Dajia Riverside Park

Lin Antai Historic House

Xinsheng Park

Taipei Arts Park

Taipei Expo Park

Bao'an Temple

Tamsui River

Keelung Chengde Bridge

Singjiang Bridge

Zhongshan Bridge

Fine Arts Museum

Sun Yat-sen Fwy

Sun Yat-sen Fwy

Jianguo N Rd

Jianguo N Rd

Minzu E Rd

Songjiang Rd

Nong'An St

Songjiang Rd

Xingtian Temple

Songjiang Rd Lane 297

Jinzou St

Minquan E Rd

Zhongquan St

Dehui St

Jilin Rd

Xinsheng N Rd

Zhongshan N Rd

Zhongshan N Rd

Minzu W Rd

Shuangcheng St Lane 28

Zhongshan Elementary School

Minquan E Rd

Jinzou St

Jinxi St

Minquan West Rd

Minquan W Rd

Minzu W Rd, Lane 32

Minzu W Rd

Dalong St Lane 215

Dalong St

Dalong Rd

Chengde Rd, Lane 285

Fushun St Lane 41

Yuanshan

Dalong Rd

Hami St

Juiquan St

Confucius Temple

Chongqing N Rd

Dalong St Lane 91

Dihua St Lane 268

Minzu W Rd

Changji St

Dihua St

Liangzhou St

Guisui St

Jinxi St

Daqiaotou

Beian Rd

500 m
0.25 miles

6
16
12
20
8
7
5
1
13
31
34
11
32

Jianguo Rd

Jianguo N Rd

26

Minsheng E Rd

10

37

Edison
Travel
Service

Jilin Rd

Changchun Rd

Yitong St

Miniatures
Museum 2
of Taiwan

Songjiang-
Nanjing

Songjiang Rd

Chang'an E Rd

3 17

Su Ho
Paper Museum

Songjiang Rd

Civic Blvd

Nanjing E Rd

Songjiang Rd Lane 85

Xinsheng Elevated Pass

Xinsheng N Rd

Minsheng E Rd

Linsen N Rd

Linsen
Park

Chang'an E Rd

22

Linsen N Rd

Civic Blvd

Zhongxiao E Rd Section 4

Jinshan S Rd

Hangzhou S Rd

Shaoxing S Rd

Zhongshan N Rd

Shuanglian

23

Lane 46

30

Nanjing W Rd

Zhongshan

19

Museum of
Contemporary Art
Taipei

Tianjin St

Beiping E Rd

Shandao
Temple

Linsen S Rd

Shaoxing S Rd

Minsheng Rd

Chengde Rd

Chang'an W Rd

Huayin St

Gongyuan Rd

Taipei
Main
Station

Zhongshan S Rd

Jingxia St

5 27

Taipei
Circle

Taiyuan Rd

Chongqing N Rd

Minsheng W Rd

Chang'an W Rd

Nanjing W Rd

Minle St

DATONG

35

25

Minle St

Dihua
Street

33

29

18

Minsheng W Rd

28

Xining N Rd

Nanjing W Rd

Chang'an W Rd

Civic Blvd

Beiman

36

Xiahai
City God
Temple

9

Dihua St

Dihua St

21

For reviews see

◉ Top Sights	p42
◉ Sights	p48
⊗ Eating	p51
◌ Drinking	p54
🎭 Entertainment	p56
🛍 Shopping	p58

Sights

Confucius Temple CONFUCIAN TEMPLE

1 Map p46, B2

Constructed by the famous Fujian craftsman Wang Yi-shun in the late 1920s, this temple is a beautiful example of Minnan (southern) architecture and of Taiwan's delightful local decorative arts. Throughout the temple there are informative displays (in English) on the history of Confucius, the temple and the Six Confucian Arts (such as archery and riding), many of which are interactive and fun for inquisitive children. (孔廟, Kǒng Miào; www.ct.taipei.gov.tw; 275 Dalong Rd; 大龍街275號; admission free; ⊙8.30am-9pm Tue-Sat, to 5pm Sun; 🚻; MYuanshan)

Miniatures Museum of Taiwan MUSEUM

2 Map p46, E6

Whimsical, wondrous and fantastically detailed are the creative works at this delightful private museum located in the basement of a nondescript tower block. On display are dozens of doll's-house-sized replications of Western houses, castles, chalets, palaces and villages, as well as scenes from classic children's stories such as *Pinocchio* and *Alice in Wonderland*. (袖珍博物館; Xiùzhēn Bówùguǎn; www.mmot.com.tw; 96 Jianguo N Rd, Sec 1; 建國北路一段96號; adult/child NT$180/100; ⊙10am-6pm Tue-Sun; MSongjiang Nanjing)

Su Ho Paper Museum MUSEUM

3 Map p46, E7

Fulfilling the lifelong dream of Taiwanese paper-maker Chen Su Ho, this stylish four-storey museum displays a working traditional paper mill and temporary exhibits (with a focus on paper sculpture and installation art), as well as good overviews of paper making around the world and in Taiwan. For a DIY experience, join the daily paper-making classes at 10am, 11am, 2pm and 3pm. (樹火紀念紙博物館; Shùhuǒ Jiniàn Zhǐ Bówùguǎn; ☎02-2507 5539; www.suhopaper.org.tw; 68 Chang'an E Rd, Sec 2; 長安東路二段68號; NT$100, with paper-making session NT$180; ⊙9.30am-4.30pm Mon-Sat; MSongjiang Nanjing)

Museum of Contemporary Art Taipei ARTS CENTRE

4 Map p46, B6

Very bright, very modern, and often fun and very experimental art is showcased here. The long red-brick building dates back to the 1920s. It started life as an elementary school and then became Taipei City Hall before its current incarnation as the city's modern art museum. Well worth a visit. Bags must be checked in. (台北當代藝術館; Táiběi Dāngdài Yìshùguǎn; ☎02-2552 3731; www.mocataipei.org.tw; 39 Chang'an W Rd; 長安西路39號; NT$50; ⊙10am-6pm Tue-Sun; MZhongshan)

Cosplayers at Taipei Expo Park

Taipei Expo Park
PARK

5 ◎ Map p46, C2

This expansive park covers three sections which are all linked up – stroll around or take a YouBike.Yuanshan Park has a lively outdoor food court (Maji Square) and the Eco Ark (a giant structure made of recycled bottles, which frequently hosts free exhibitions). Across Zhongshan N Rd you'll find the **International Pavilion of Indigenous Arts and Cultures** (原民風味館; Yuánmín Fēngwèiguǎn; www. facebook.com/Taiwan.paf; 151 Zhongshan N Rd, Sec 3;中山北路三段151號; ⊘11am-7pm Tue-Sun; P; M Yuanshan), the Fine Arts Museum (p50), and **Taipei Story House** (台北故事館; Táiběi Gùshìguǎn;

www.taipeistoryhouse.org.tw; 181-1 Zhongshan N Rd, Sec 3; 中山北路三段181之1號; NT$50; ⊘10am-5.30pm Tue-Sun; P; M Yuanshan). Further east, Xinsheng Park has innovative pavilions and Lin Antai Historic House (p50). (花博公園; Huàbó Gōngyuán; www.taipei-expopark. tw; P ⋔; M Yuanshan)

National Revolutionary Martyrs' Shrine
SHRINE

6 ◎ Map p46, D1

This large shrine marks the memory of almost 400,000 soldiers who died for the ROC (mostly within China). The bulky complex, built in 1969, is typical of the northern 'palace style' architecture popularised during

LITTLELIN / SHUTTERSTOCK ©

Understand

A Little Art Lesson

Zhongshan is home to Taipei's two best art museums, the Museum of Contemporary Art (p48) and the Fine Arts Museum (p50), which showcase the country's rich and varied art scene covering genres such as painting, film, dance, ceramics and literature. Local arts are either wholly indigenous or evolved from Chinese genres, carried over by waves of immigrants from mainland China, or a unique mix of both.

Western styles of painting were introduced to Taiwan by the Japanese. Ishikawa Kinichiro (1871–1945), now considered the father of modern Taiwanese art, taught local painters to work the tropical landscapes of Taiwan in a French impressionistic style.

During the 1970s a strong nativist movement, sometimes referred to as Taiwan Consciousness, began to develop. Artists found inspiration in Taiwanese folk traditions and the arts and crafts of indigenous tribes.

The opening of the Taipei Fine Arts Museum and the ending of martial law were two of the most significant events in the 1980s. For the first time, artists could actively criticise the political system without suffering consequences.

Chiang Kai-shek's reign. The hourly changing of the guards is a popular attraction, especially with Japanese tourists. It takes almost 20 minutes for the white-clad soldiers to march from the gate to their posts in front of the memorial, giving plenty of time to get a good photo. (國民革命忠烈祠; Guómín Géming Zhōngliècí; 139 Beian Rd; 北安路139號; admission free; ⏰9am-5pm; Dazhi)

Fine Arts Museum
MUSEUM

7 Map p46, C2

Constructed in the 1980s, this airy, four-storey box of marble, glass and concrete showcases contemporary art, with a particular focus on Taiwanese artists. Exhibits include pieces by

Taiwanese painters and sculptors from the Japanese period through to the present. Check the website to see what's currently showing. (市立美術館; Shìlì Měishùguǎn; www.tfam.museum; 181 Zhongshan N Rd, Sec 3; 中山北路三段181號; NT$50; ⏰9.30am-5.30pm Tue-Fri & Sun, to 8.30pm Sat; P; MYuanshan)

Lin Antai
Historic House
HISTORIC BUILDING

8 Map p46, D2

This Fujian-style 30-room house, Taipei's oldest residential building, was first erected between 1783 and 1787, near what is now Dunhua S Rd. As was typical in those times, the house expanded as the family grew in numbers and wealth, reaching its present size in 1823.In the 1970s, the heyday of Taiwan's 'economic miracle', the home was set to be demolished for the great purpose of road widening. Thankfully, public opinion saved the day and the house was painstakingly dismantled and, in 1983, rebuilt on this field in Xinsheng Park. (林安泰古厝, Lín Āntài Gǔ Cuò; english.linantai.taipei; 5 Binjiang St; 濱江街5號; admission free; ⏰9am-5pm Tue-Sun; MYuanshan)

Xiahai City God Temple
TAOIST TEMPLE

9 ◉ Map p46, A7

This lively and well-loved temple on Dihua St (p44) was built in 1856 to house the City God statue that the losers in the Wanhua feud took as they fled upstream. Little changed since those days, the temple is a terrific spot to witness folk worship rituals as well as admire some gorgeous pieces of traditional arts and crafts. (霞海城隍廟; Xiáhǎi Chénghuáng Miào; Hsiahai City God Temple; www.tpecitygod. org; 61 Dihua St, Sec 1; 迪化街一段61號; MZhongshan)

Edison Travel Service
TOURS

10 ◉ Map p46, E5

Edison Travel Service offers three-hour city tours (adult/child NT$1000/900) with an English-speaking guide that take in the Martyrs' Shrine, the National Palace Museum, Chiang Kai-shek Memorial Hall, a temple visit and some shopping. (☏02-2563 4621; www.edison. com.tw; 4th fl, 190 Songjiang Rd; 松江路190 號4樓; ⏰7am-11pm; MXingtian Temple)

Eating

Qing Tian Xia
CHINESE $$

11 ⊗ Map p46, A4

At the northern end of historic Dihua St is Taipei's first Guizhou restaurant. The interior is upscale but relaxed, and dishes are authentic and well presented. There's no menu; order from your smartphone or the restaurant's tablet. The restaurant is in a courtyard off the main street, just south of Minquan W Rd. (黔天下; Qián Tiānxià; ☏02-2557 7872; www.ocg.url.tw; 358-2 Dihua St, Sec 1; 迪化街一段358-2; dishes NT$150-500; ⏰11.30am-2.30pm & 5.30-9.30pm Tue-Sun; ❄🛜; MDaqiaotou)

Top Tip

City God's Birthday

On the City God's Birthday (the 14th day of the fifth lunar month), dozens of temples around Taipei send teams to Xiahai to entertain the City God. The procession stretches over a kilometre and performances include lion dances, god dances and martial arts displays. Things get going around 2pm to 3pm and all the festivities last five days. See Xiahai's website (www.tpecitygod.org) for more information.

Addiction Aquatic Development

SEAFOOD $$

12 Map p46, E3

Housed in the former Taipei Fish Market – you can't miss it, it's a huge blue and slate-grey building – is this collection of chic eateries serving the freshest seafood imaginable. There's a stand-up sushi bar, a seafood bar (with wine available), hotpot, an outdoor grill, a wholesale area for take-home seafood and a lifestyle boutique. This place is popular and doesn't take reservations. (上引水產; Shàng Yǐn Shuǐchǎn; www.addiction.com.tw; 18, Alley 2, Lane 410, Minzu E Rd; 民族東路410巷2弄18號; ☉10am-midnight; Ⓜ Xingtian Temple)

#21 Goose & Seafood

TAIWANESE $

13 Map p46, C4

Loud, rustic and fun, 21 offers great food in a genuine Taiwanese environment (you sit on little bamboo benches in an open shop, facing the street). The place gets its name from its two specialities: roasted goose meat and an assortment of fried and stewed fish dishes. (21號鵝肉海鮮; 21 Hào É'ròu Hǎixiān; ☎02-2536 2121; 21 Jinzou St; 錦州街21號; dishes NT$40-150; ☉5pm-4am; Ⓜ Zhongshan Elementary School)

Yangzhou Guan Tangbao

DUMPLING $

14 Map p46, E7

An excellent value, family-run restaurant serving some of the city's best *tāng bāo* (湯包; thick dumplings filled with a soupy broth in addition to meat and veggies). A steamer holds eight dumplings. Pair them with some savoury lamb soup (羊肉清湯; *yángròu qīngtāng*). (揚州灌湯包; Yángzhōu Guàn Tāngbāo; ☎02-8772 3580; 284 Bade Rd, Sec 2; 八德路二段284號; *tāng bāo* NT$90; ☉11am-9pm Tue-Sun; Ⓜ Nanjing Fuxing)

Ningxia Night Market

MARKET $

15 Map p46, B5

This is an excellent venue for sampling traditional snacks, not least because the street is not cramped and most stalls have tables. The food here is very fresh, and dishes to try include fish soup, oyster omelette, satay beef, sweet peanut soup (花生湯; *huāshēng tāng*) and fried taro cake (芋餅; *yùbǐng*). If you are brave try the bitter tea (苦茶; *kǔchá*). (寧夏夜市; Níngxià Yèshì; cnr Ningxia & Nanjing W Rds; ☉6am-midnight; Ⓜ Zhongshan)

RAW

MODERN FRENCH $$$

16 Map p46, E1

RAW is all the rage in Taipei. You'll need to make reservations a month in advance for this place, owned by Taiwanese celebrity chef Andre Chiang. Multicourse set dinners of concept food have been variously called imaginative, creative, multiflavoured and perfectly presented. The decor matches the decadent air, with secret drawers and a boat-shaped bar. (☎02-8501 5800; www.raw.com.tw; 301 Lequn

Parade for Xiahai City God, whose primary temple (p51) is found on Dihua St

Rd, Sec 3; 樂群路三段301號; per person NT$1850; ☉11.30am-2.30pm & 6-10pm Wed-Sun; ✳; Ⓜ Jiannan Rd)

Old Sichuan

SICHUAN $$$

17 Map p46, E7

As soon as you walk in you can smell the Sichuan peppercorns and hot oil. Old Sichuan is a theatrical experience, from the decor, which is over-the-top red-and-gold imperial den, to the fiery spicy hotpots. Famous locally and among the tourist set; if you've got the budget, this is a must-visit. (老 四川; Lǎo Sìchuān; ☎02-2515 2222; www. oldsichuan.com.tw; 112 Chang'an E Rd, Sec 2; 長安東路二段112號; ☉11.30am-1.30am; ✳; Ⓜ Songjiang-Nanjing)

Salt Peanuts

CAFE $$

18 Map p46, A5

Although it feels more like a coffee parlour, Salt Peanuts offers inventive brunch sets with delicately dressed salads, toasted tofu sandwiches and chunky vegetable quiches. The inner courtyard garden is a real treat with lush trees and ferns and tiled flooring. You won't want to take photos of the food here, as you'll be more interested in your surroundings. (鹹 花生; Xián Huāshēng; ☎02-2557 8679; 197 Dihua St, Sec 1; 迪化街一段197號; lunch sets NT$270-300; ✳ ⓦ; Ⓜ Shuanglian)

Shin Yeh

TAIWANESE $$$

19 Map p46, C6

This well-regarded chain serves up traditional Taiwanese food in an upmarket environment. Try the fried tofu, stewed pork or fried oysters. The restaurant is located on the 8th floor of building one of the Shin Kong Mitsukoshi Department Store (take exit 2). (欣葉台菜; Xīnyè Táicài; ☑02-2523 6757; www.shinyeh.com.tw; 8th fl, 12 Nanjing W Rd; 南京西路12號8樓; dishes NT$290-580; ⏲11.30am-4pm & 5-8.30pm; ❄❂; Ⓜ Zhongshan)

Paris 1930

FRENCH $$$

20 Map p46, D4

This restaurant in the Landis Hotel is consistently rated as having the best French food in town and is also one of the fanciest dining experiences on offer. Diners must wear smart clothing and switch phones to silent. Reservations are recommended. (巴黎廳; Bālítīng; ☑02-2597 1234; taipei.landishotelsresorts.com; 2nd fl, 41 Minquan E Rd, Sec 2; 民權東路二段41號2樓; meals NT$2800-3600; ⏲6-10pm daily & 11.30am-2pm Sat & Sun; Ⓜ Zhongshan Elementary School)

Drinking

Lugou Cafe

CAFE

21 Map p46, A8

Speciality coffees (including some local choices such as Alishan) in a heritage building (originally the chemist A S Watson & Co) on Dihua St.

Mismatched furniture, eclectic decor, Frank Sinatra jazz: grab a window seat and step back in time. The coffee is a pleasure, the sandwiches not so. (爐鍋咖啡; Lúguō Kāfēi; ☑02-2555 8225; www.facebook.com/luguocafeartyard; 1, 2nd fl, Lane 32, Dihua St, Sec 1; 迪化街一段32巷1號2樓; ⏲11am-7pm; ❂; Ⓜ Zhongshan)

Goldfish

GAY

22 Map p46, C6

Nice cocktail bar with inventive recipes in the Japanese quarter. Popular with bears and muscled types. (☑02-2581 3133; www.facebook.com/goldfishtaipei; 13, Lane 85, Linsen N Rd; 林森北路85巷13號; ⏲9pm-late; ❂; Ⓜ Shandao Temple)

Dance Cafe

CAFE

23 Map p46, C5

Elegant, serene and loaded with history, this cafe is located in a former wooden dormitory (with a large deck spilling on to a grassy lawn) built by the Japanese in 1925. Next door is the Tsai Jui-yueh dance studio and together the cafe and studio are known as the Rose Heritage Site. Tsai was a pioneer of modern dance in Taiwan. (玫瑰古蹟跳舞咖啡廳; Méiguī Gǔjī Tiàowǔ Kāfēi Tīng; 1, Lane 46, Zhongshan N Rd, Sec 2; 中山北路2段46巷1號; ⏲10am-10pm; ❂; Ⓜ Shuanglian)

G*Star Club

GAY

24 Map p46, E7

A crazy crowd of mainly young Taiwanese guys. The club is very active in terms of events and parties.

Understand

Religion in Taiwan

- -

A Brief History

Early immigrants to Taiwan faced conditions not unlike those faced by settlers in the New World: a harsh environment, hostile natives and a host of devastating diseases. Faith in the local cults of their home village in China was vital in forming new and strong community bonds in Taiwan.

During the late Qing dynasty and into Japanese times, a period of increasing wealth and mobility, many temples began to expand their influence beyond the village level. Famous pilgrim sites arose, and Matsu (goddess of seafarers) started her rise to pan-Taiwan deity status.

Pick 'n' Mix

The Taiwanese approach to spirituality is eclectic and not particularly dogmatic; many Taiwanese will combine elements from various religions to suit their needs rather than rigidly adhering to one particular spiritual path. Religion in Taiwan is largely about an individual relationship to a deity, dead spirit or even spiritual leader. Many of the gods, customs and festivals are sometimes described as part of an amorphous folk faith. But don't expect anyone to ever tell you they are a believer in this faith: instead, they will say they are Taoist or Buddhist.

Folk Religion

Beliefs about ancestor worship permeate almost every aspect of Chinese philosophy. Most homes in Taiwan have their own altar, where family members pay their respects to deceased relatives by burning incense and providing offerings.

Closely tied to ancestor worship is popular or folk religion, which consists of an immense celestial bureaucracy of gods and spirits, from the lowly but important kitchen god (*zào jūn*) to the celestial emperor himself (*tiāndì* or *shàngdì*). Like the imperial bureaucrats on earth, each god has a particular role to fulfil and can be either promoted or demoted depending on his or her job performance. Offerings to the gods consist not only of food and incense, but also opera performances, birthday parties (to which other local gods are invited) and even processions around town.

Drinks are not overpriced. (📞02-2721 8323; www.facebook.com/gstarclub; B1, 23, Longjiang Rd; 龍江路23號; ⏰10pm-late; Ⓜ Nanjing Fuxing)

Le Zinc
WINE BAR

25 🚇 Map p46, A7

This warm and stylish cafe/wine bar is set at the far back of one of Dihua St's traditional brick shops (originally a medicine shop built in 1923). Enter via Artyard67 (p59), a wonderful ceramic studio, to get a look at how these very long and narrow buildings were constructed to facilitate air flow and natural lighting. If you arrive late, enter from the back alley. (www.facebook.com/lezinclo; 67 Dihua St, Sec 1; 迪化街一段67號; ⏰10am-7pm Sun & Mon, to midnight Tue-Sat; 📶; Ⓜ Zhongshan)

Local Life
Taipei's Eye
Miramar Entertainment Park (美麗華百樂園; Měilìhuá Bǎilèyuán; www.miramar.com.tw; tickets Mon-Fri NT$150, Sat & Sun NT$200; ⏰11am-11pm Sun-Thu, to midnight Fri & Sat; Ⓜ Jiannan Rd) is part mall, part amusement park, all fun. It's a huge attraction for local families with its slowly-rotating 100m-tall Ferris wheel, located on the roof. There are panoramic views and, of course, plenty of things to eat in Miramar's fine food court, and there's a giant IMAX cinema screen.

Taboo
LESBIAN

26 🚇 Map p46, E5

This lesbian club attracts a very young set of girls, with the liveliest nights Friday and Saturday. There's a dance floor and DJ. For women, it's NT$300 to NT$500 to get in, with free drinks all night. This encourages rather a lot of drinking. For men, entry is NT$700 or more, depending on the event. Taboo often has theme parties: those who dress up get in cheaper. Be sure to bring your ID! (www.taboo.com.tw; 90 Jianguo N Rd, Sec 2; 建國北路二段90號; ⏰7pm-1am Wed & Thu, 10pm-4am Fri & Sat; Ⓜ Xingtian Temple)

ANIKi Club
GAY

27 🚇 Map p46, B5

This gay sauna remains one of the most popular saunas with younger men. It has great facilities, is clean and modern, and includes a gym. (www.aniki.com.tw; 11 Ningxia Rd; 寧夏路11號; 16hr NT$1000; ⏰24hr; 📶; Ⓜ Zhongshan)

Entertainment

Taiyuan Asian Puppet Theatre Museum
PUPPET THEATRE

28 ⭐ Map p46, A5

A combination interactive museum, workshop and theatre, this complex is a must-visit for anyone interested in traditional performing arts. For starters, the Asian puppet collection here is the largest in the world. There

Miramar Entertainment Park

are also two puppetry troupes who regularly perform both here and internationally. All performances have English subtitles projected on a screen. (台原亞洲偶戲博物館; Táiyuán Yàzhōu Ôuxì Bówùguǎn; ☎02-2556 8909; www.taipeipuppet.com; 79 Xining N Rd; 西寧 北路79號; museum adult/child NT$80/50; ⊙10am-5pm Tue-Sun; Ⓜ Daqiaotou)

Dadaocheng Theatre OPERA

29 ⭐ Map p46, B8

Above the Yongle Market, this theatre regularly holds performances of Taiwanese opera. In May and June it hosts free shows in the outside square. To find the elevators to the 8th floor, look for the entrance to the right as you face the market. (大稻 埕戲苑; Dàdàochéng Xìyuàn; ☎02-2556 9101; www.facebook.com/dadaochen2011; 8th & 9th fl, 21 Dihua St, Sec 1; 迪化街一 段21號8-9樓; ⊙9am-5.30pm Tue-Sun; Ⓜ Zhongshan)

SPOT – Taipei Film House CINEMA

30 ⭐ Map p46, C5

This excellent art-house cinema is in a beautiful white colonial building that was once home to the US ambassador, and which dates back to 1925. The leafy garden has a cafe, a perfect place for a post-film chilled glass of white wine in summer. There is also a branch of SPOT at Huashan

1914 Creative Park (p26). (光點台北; Guāngdiǎn Táiběi; ☎02-2511 7786; www.spot.org.tw; 18 Zhongshan N Rd, Sec 2; 中山北路二段18號; tickets NT$260; ◷11am-10pm; ⓂZhongshan)

Taipei Eye

PERFORMING ARTS

31 ☆ Map p46, C4

Taipei Eye showcases Chinese opera together with other rotating performances, including puppet theatre and indigenous dance. This is a tourist show, but it's well regarded and booking can be done online in English. There are three to four shows weekly, usually starting around 8pm. (台北戲棚; Táiběi Xìpéng; ☎02-2568 2677; www.taipeieye.com; 113 Zhongshan N Rd, Sec 2; 中山北路二段113號; tickets Mon, Wed & Fri NT$550, Sat NT$880; ⓂShuanglian)

Shopping

Lao Mian Cheng Lantern Shop

HANDICRAFTS

32 🔒 Map p46, A4

Handmade lamps, with painted dragons, bold flowers, bamboo and calligraphy, are solid red, and as big as a gym ball or small as a fist. There are also concertinaed paper lanterns, purses and cushion covers. This tumbledown marvel of a shop was opened back in 1915 by the current owner's grandfather. It's usually closed on Sunday. (老面成, Lǎomiànchéng; 298 Dihua St, Sec 1; 迪化街一段298號; ◷9am-8pm Mon-Sat; ⓂDaqiaotou)

Yongle Market

MARKET

33 🔒 Map p46, B8

The rather ugly concrete structure, grafted on to a beautiful colonial-era facade adjacent to Dadaocheng Theatre (p57), houses a huge fabric market on the 2nd floor. Cotton, satin, silk, gauze, Japanese prints, bold colours, cat or owl designs, stripes, gingham and feather boas – bolts and bolts of it. Fabric is sold by the *chi* (尺), about 30cm, or *ma* (碼), 90cm. (永樂市場; Yǒnglè Shìchǎng; 21 Dihua St, Sec 1; 迪化街一段21號; ◷10am-6pm Mon-Sat; ⓂZhongshan)

Lin Hua Tai Tea Company

TEA

34 🔒 Map p46, B4

The oldest tea-selling shop in Taipei, dating back to 1883. The current fourth-generation merchants are more than happy to talk tea and let you sample the wares, which sit in large metal drums about the warehouse. Prices per *jin* (600g) are clearly written on the top of each drum. Ask for a tour of the tea factory at the back. (林華泰茶行; Línhuátài Cháháng; ☎02-2557 3506; 193 Chongqing N Rd, Sec 2; 重慶北路二段193號; ◷7.30am-9pm; ⓂDaqiaotou)

in Bloooom

ARTS & CRAFTS

35 🔒 Map p46, B7

This funky fabric shop uses bold and bright designs in cotton canvas to make bags, purses, laptop cases, book covers, Japanese wall curtains and anything you like. One of in Bloom's hallmark motifs is repeated mynah

Opera performance at Taipei Eye

birds in silhouette. You can also have any item custom-made with their fabric. (印花樂; Yìnhuālè; ☎02-2555 1026; www.inblooom.com; 28 Minle St; 民樂街28號; ◷9.30am-7pm; Ⓜ Zhongshan)

ArtYard67 CERAMICS

36 🔒 Map p46, A7

In a restored long shophouse from 1923, this exceptional ceramic studio carries the Hakka Blue brand, inspired by the indigo colour of Hakka clothing. (民藝埕67; Mínyìchéng Liùshíqī; ☎02-2552 1367; 67 Dihua St, Sec 1; 迪化街一段67號; ◷10am-7pm; Ⓜ Zhongshan)

Ten Shang's Tea Company TEA

37 🔒 Map p46, D5

Hailing from a mountain tea-growing community in central Taiwan's Nantou, Mr and Mrs Chang have been selling organically grown oolong teas from all over Taiwan for a quarter of a century. Visitors are welcome to come in and chat over a pot or two of their exquisite high-mountain tea while shopping for tea and supplies. (天样茗茶; Tiānshàng Míngchá; ☎02-2542 6542; 156 Jilin Rd; 吉林路156號; ◷10am-10pm Mon-Sat, 2-10pm Sun; Ⓜ Xingtian Temple)

Explore

Ximending & Wanhua

Wanhua is where Taipei first started out as a trading centre, growing rich selling tea, coal and camphor. Today this area is a window on history, with its temples and heritage buildings. Just to the north is the Ximending (西門町; Xīméndīng; Ximen) pedestrian district, dripping with a Japanese youth consumer vibe and chock-full of young couples, fast food, cinemas and shops selling novelties, cosmetics and clothing.

The Sights in a Day

☀ The best time to visit a temple is in the early morning and **Longshan** (p63) is no exception. Watch the locals pray for a partner, a baby, or a good exam result and then cleanse your vital organs with a cup of bitter tea from Herb Alley. Wind your way north, making sure to take in the heritage street of **Bopiliao** (p65) and the leafy stillness of **Qingshan Temple** (p64).

☀ By the time you get to Ximen (pictured left) it will be time for lunch. Queue up for street-side slurping at **Ay-Chung** (p65) or head underground for nationalist noodles at **Lao Shan Dong** (p66). Spend the afternoon exploring the lanes of cute shops; break for a coffee in famous **Fong Da** (p67).

☾ Ximen really comes alive at night. If you like the boisterous gay crowd the **Red House Bar Street** (p67) not only has killer cocktails but also an excellent al fresco Thai restaurant, **Thai Food** (p65). Otherwise, inflame your taste buds with fiery Sichuan fare at **Zhen Siwei** (p65).

 Best of Taipei

Best History
Zhongshan Hall (p63)

Bopiliao (p65)

Best Cafes & Teahouses
Fong Da Coffee (p67)

Eighty-Eightea (p68)

Best Bars
Red House Bar Street (p67)

Getting There

Ⓜ **MRT** These two districts are easily accessed from the blue line between Longshan Temple and Ximen.

For reviews see

RICHIE CHAN / SHUTTERSTOCK ©

Zhongshan Hall

Sights

Longshan Temple BUDDHIST TEMPLE

1 ◉ Map p62, A5

Founded in 1738 by Han immigrants from Fujian, this temple has served as a municipal, guild and self-defence centre, as well as a house of worship. These days it is one of the city's top religious sites, and a prime venue for exploring both Taiwan's vibrant folk faith and its unique temple arts and architecture. (龍山寺; Lóngshān Sì; www.lungshan.org.tw; 211 Guangzhou St; 廣州街211號; ⊙6am-10pm; Ⓜ Longshan Temple)

Zhongshan Hall HISTORIC BUILDING

2 ◉ Map p62, D3

This four-storey building, constructed in 1936 for the coronation of Emperor Hirohito, is where the Japanese surrender ceremony was held in October 1945, and later where Chiang Kai-shek delivered speeches from the terrace following his four 're-elections'. The 3rd-floor tearoom contains the masterwork *Water Buffalo* by Huang Tu-shui (1895–1930), the first Taiwanese artist to study in Japan. (中山堂; Zhōngshān Táng; ☏02-2381 3137; http://english.zsh.taipei.gov.tw; 98 Yanping S Rd; 延平南路98號; admission free; ⊙9.30am-9pm; Ⓜ Ximen)

Red House

CULTURAL CENTRE

3 💿 Map p62, C3

Ximending's most iconic building was built in 1908 to serve as Taipei's first public market. These days it's a multifunctional cultural centre with regular live performances and exhibitions. There's an artist and designer weekend market in the north square (2pm to 9.30pm Saturday and Sunday), and 16 studios selling the works of local designers (2pm to 9.30pm Tuesday to Sunday) behind the main entrance. (西門紅樓; Xīmén Hónglóu; ☑02-2311 9380; www.redhouse.org.tw; 10 Chengdu Rd; 成都路10號; ⏰11am-9.30pm Tue-Sun; Ⓜ Ximen)

Qingshan Temple

TAOIST TEMPLE

4 💿 Map p62, A4

Along with Longshan, this elegant temple, first built in 1856, is one of Wanhua's top houses of worship. There is an abundance of top-quality wood, stone and decorative artwork to see here and the **god's birthday festival** is one of Taipei liveliest religious events. Called the **Night Patrol** (夜間出巡; Yèjiān Chūxún), this parade takes place from 5pm to 9pm over two nights (the 20th and 21st days of the lunar 10th month; around the end of November or early December). (青山宮; Qīngshān Gōng; 218 Guiyang St, Sec 2; 貴陽街二段218號; ⏰5.30am-9pm; Ⓜ Longshan)

Understand

The Lowdown on Longshan

Longshan is dedicated to the Bodhisattva of mercy, Guanyin, though in true Taiwanese style there are over 100 other gods and goddesses worshipped in the rear and side halls. Matsu, goddess of the sea, is enshrined in the back centre; Wenchang Dijun, the god of literature, to the far right (come during exam period to see how important he is); red-faced Guan Gong, the god of war and patron of police and gangsters, is enshrined to the far left; and in front of that is the Old Man Under the Moon, known as the Matchmaker or the Chinese cupid.

Check out the two-of-a-kind bronze pillars outside the front hall and the incense holders outside the main hall. The handles depict a common temple motif: The Fool Holding up the Sky. The Western-style appearance of the 'fools' is no coincidence. They are said to represent the Dutch, who occupied Taiwan in the 17th century.

The best times to visit Longshan are around 6am, 8am and 5pm, when crowds of worshippers gather and engage in hypnotic chanting.

Bopiliao   AREA

5 ⊙ Map p62, A5

One of the best-preserved historic sections of Wanhua, Bopiliao covers both Qing and early Japanese-era architecture. Some of the buildings house art galleries (generally open from 9am to 6pm, Tuesday to Sunday) showing experimental works mostly by young local artists. Bopiliao isn't as atmospheric as Dihua St (p44) because there's no living history left, but it's worth a look if you're in the area. It's just up from the corner of Kangding and Guangzhou Sts. (剝皮寮; Bō Pí Liáo; ⊙9am-9pm; Ⓜ Longshan Temple)

Eating

Thai Food   THAI $

6 ✗ Map p62, C3

Don't overlook this unassuming place in the far corner of the courtyard behind the Red House. Basically a one-woman show (a Chinese lady born in Thailand), Thai Food serves some of the most authentic and delicious curries, soups and salads in Taipei and at rock-bottom prices. Two types of Thai beer (NT$80) are also on offer. (泰風味; Tài Fēngwèi; 25, Lane 10, Chengdu Rd; 成都路10巷25號; dishes NT$100-300; ⊙2-10pm Tue-Sun; Ⓜ Ximen)

◯ Local Life
Hidden Temple

Tianhou Temple (天后宮; Tiānhòu Gōng; 51 Chengdu Rd; 成都路51號; admission free; ⊙6am-10pm; Ⓜ Ximen) is a small, atmospheric temple that appears from the outside to be a narrow, elaborate shopfront in the Ximending area. But walk through the gate and you'll find one of Taipei's most intriguing temples, a place where Japanese and Chinese worship patterns existed, and still exist, side by side.

Zhen Siwei   SICHUAN $$

7 ✗ Map p62, B2

Lane 25 is packed with Sichuan restaurants, and this one, at the head of the lane, has the craziest queues. No-nonsense authentic Sichuan fare. (真四味, Zhēnsìwèi; 39-1, Lane 25, Kangding Rd; 康定路25巷39-1號; dishes NT$120-300; ⊙11am-2pm & 5-9pm Tue-Sun; ✳; Ⓜ Ximen)

Ay-Chung Flour Rice Noodle   NOODLES $

8 ✗ Map p62, C3

You can spot this place by the huge crowds eating noodles outside. The slurpalicious, salty noodles are very appealing on a cool Taipei evening. (阿宗麵線; Ā Zōng Miànxiàn; 8-1 Emei St; 峨嵋街8之1號; noodles NT$50-65; ⊙9.30am-10.30pm Mon-Thu, to 11pm Fri-Sun; Ⓜ Ximen)

Understand
Pictures & Popcorn

Ximending is the place to head for a large variety of films; there's a cluster of movie theatres along Wucheng St. Other leading multiplexes are Vieshow Cinemas (p103) in Xinyi District and Breeze Centre's Ambassador Theatre (p95). Taipei's most respected art-house cinema is SPOT – Taipei Film House (p57). There is also a branch of SPOT at Huashan 1914 Creative Park (p26), while the Eslite Spectrum (p110) has a secret little art-house cinema.

Tickets are generally NT$250-300. English-language films (except sometimes cartoons) are in English. Chinese-language films are often subtitled in English.

Lao Shan Dong Homemade Noodles

NOODLES $

9 Map p62, C2

Super popular with locals, this unpretentious canteen has been serving up handmade, thick, floury, Shandong-style noodles – you can watch the noodle-makers in their puffs of flour while you eat – since it opened in 1949 (a momentous year for Taiwan!). The noodles are firm and bouncy and the broth is light and tangy. The English menu is handwritten in a child's schoolbook. (老山東牛肉家常麵店; Lǎoshāndōng Niúròu Jiācháng Miàndiàn; Shop 15,

basement, 70 Xining S Rd; 西寧南路70號地下室15; noodles from NT$80; ◷11am-10pm; ✳; ⓂXimen)

Dongyi Paigu

TAIWANESE $

10 Map p62, D2

Disco lives – or at least glitter balls, mirrored walls and stained-glass ceilings do – at this flashy but friendly place specialising in simple, well-prepared *páigǔ fàn* (排骨飯; pork with rice). There's no English menu, but the pictures on the wall are enough. The serving ladies in white smocks are straight out of the 1960s and super smiley. Well worth it for the atmosphere. (東一排骨總店; Dōngyī Páigǔ Zǒngdiàn; ☎02-2381 1487; 2nd fl, 61 Yanping S Rd; 延平南路61號2樓; rice dishes NT$140-170; ◷10am-8.45pm Tue-Sun; ✳; ⓂXimen)

Dai Sya Rinn Restaurant

JAPANESE $$

11 Map p62, C2

Plates of raw fish and assorted sushi are pulled past customers by tiny trains and Taiwanese pop music from the '50s fills the air in this fun throwback to a time when Emei St was a major commercial centre. Taipei's first conveyor-belt sushi joint, it still serves first-rate seafood in this narrow, near-subterranean hideout. (大車輪餐飲企業; Dà Chēlún Cānyǐn Qǐyè; Da Che Lun; www.dsr.tw; 53 Emei St; 峨嵋街53號; dishes from NT$180; ◷11am-9.30pm; ✳; ⓂXimen)

NATTAWIT JEERAPATMAITREE / SHUTTERSTOCK ©

Red House (p64)

Drinking

Red House Bar Street   GAY

This strip of open-air bars (see 3  Map p62, C3) behind the historic Red House is a friendly and lively gay district that welcomes everyone. You will often see families with children mixing with the camp crowd. (Behind the Red House; ⏰6pm-late; 📶; Ⓜ Ximen)

Fong Da Coffee   CAFE

12 Ⓠ Map p62, C3

One of Taipei's original coffee shops, Fong Da dates from 1956 and still uses some of the original equipment. It's always bustling, testament to the great brews to be had here. It's also a great place to buy whole beans or coffee-brewing devices such as siphons or Italian stovetop espresso makers. (蜂大咖啡; Fēngdà Kāfēi; 📞02-2371 9577; 42 Chengdu Rd; 成都路42號; ⏰8am-10pm; Ⓜ Ximen)

Herb Alley   TRADITIONAL DRINKS

13 Ⓠ Map p62, A5

Just around the corner from Longshan Temple is this herb-selling area that dates back to Qing times. It's a great place to sample some of the incredible range of Chinese herbal drinks available, though some may truly curdle your liver. (青草巷; Qīngcǎo Xiàng; Lane 224, Xichang St; 西昌路224巷; drinks NT$15-50; ⏰9am-10pm; Ⓜ Longshan Temple)

Top Tip

Bargain Beauty

If you're after cheap beauty treatments, you're in luck: the shops along Zhongshan Rd near Ximen MRT exit 6 offer some of the lowest cost gel services in the city. A soft gel manicure, for example, costs around NT$300 and eyebrow shaping just NT$100. They are always packed with young Taiwanese women.

Eighty-Eightea   TEAHOUSE

14 Map p62, C4

Housed in the refurbished wooden quarters of a Japanese priest, this lovely teahouse really catches the afternoon light through its windows. There's a Japanese sitting area, as well as regular tables, where you can enjoy one of the house-branded Taiwanese teas. Simple rice dishes are also available. (八拾捌茶; Bāshíbā Chá; ☏02-2312 0845; www.eightyeightea.com; Xibenyuan Temple Sq, cnr Changsha St & Zhonghua Rd; ⏰1-9pm Mon-Fri, 10.30am-9pm Sat & Sun; ☏; Ⓜ Ximen)

Somebody Cafe   CAFE

15 Map p62, C3

This bright design cafe has sanded school desks for tables and is decorated with its signature black-line drawings. It also sells cushions and notebooks with the distinctive patterns. A perfect place to escape the shopping madness of Ximending below. (2nd fl, 65 Chengdu Rd; 成都路65號2樓; ⏰10am-10pm; ☏; Ⓜ Ximen)

Le Promenoir Coffee   CAFE

16 Map p62, D3

This cafe is set in a long gallery on the 4th floor of Zhongshan Hall. It's the perfect setting for reading or meeting a friend. Look out for the magnificent green grand piano with the painted peacocks. (4f劇場咖啡; 4F Jùchǎng Kāfēi; 4th fl, 98 Yanping South Rd; 延平南路98號4樓l; ⏰11am-9pm; ☏; Ⓜ Ximen)

Rainbow Sauna   GAY

17 Map p62, B3

One of Taipei's oldest gay saunas and still going strong. A bit dark and grungy now, but popular with younger guys because it's cheaper. (彩虹會館; Cǎihóng Huìguǎn; 2nd fl, 142 Kunming St; 昆明街142號2樓; ⏰24hr; Ⓜ Ximen)

Entertainment

PartyWorld   KARAOKE

18 Map p62, D3

This outlet of the popular chain of karaokes with private room rentals is in the Ximending area. (錢櫃; Qiánguì; www.cashboxparty.com; 55 Zhonghua Rd, Sec 1; 中華路一段55號; ⏰24hr; ☏; Ⓜ Ximen)

Riverside Live House   LIVE MUSIC

19 Map p62, C3

One of Taipei's best live venues, the 800-seat Riverside sits behind the historic Red House (p64) in Ximending. Acts range from local Mandopop (Mandarin pop music) to jazz and straight-

Ximending pedestrian district

on rock and roll. (河岸留言; Hé'àn Liúyán; ☎02-2370 8805; www.riverside.com.tw; 177 Xining S Rd; 西寧南路177號; MXimen)

Shopping

Forbidden
ADULT

20 🔒 Map p62, C3

One of the best sex shops in the gay bar district, selling underwear, swimwear, T-shirts, lube, condoms, sex toys and one of Taiwan's craziest novelty souvenirs – a giant penis pineapple cake (also comes in other flavours, such as blueberry and passionfruit). (21, Lane 10, Chengdu Rd; 成都路10巷21號; ⊙1pm-midnight; MXimen)

Little Garden Embroidered Shoes
SHOES

21 🔒 Map p62, B2

This third-generation shop is the last remaining traditional embroidered-shoe outlet in Taipei. Most of the dainty little items (with patterns such as auspicious dragons, peonies and phoenixes) are now made with computer-controlled machines, but you can still order completely hand-stitched ones. Shoes start at NT$690. (小花園; Xiǎohuāyuán; ☎02-2311 0045; www.taipei-shoes.com; 70 Emei St; 峨嵋街 70號; ⊙12.30-6pm; MXimen)

Explore

Da'an

Da'an (大安; Dà'ān) is an important commercial and residential area (property prices are among the highest in the city) with several major universities. It's not big on sights – it's a new district after all – but this is where you'll find some of Taipei's ritziest shopping areas, some of its top restaurants, and, best of all, there is lovely leafy Da'an Park.

The Sights in a Day

☀ Start your morning with a gentle stroll in **Da'an Forest Park** (p76; pictured left) with Taipei's affluent as they jog or walk their dogs in this green oasis. At the southwest corner is the curious **Taipei Grand Mosque** (p76). It's at its most liveliest during Friday prayers. Take your coffee and brunch in vintage style at **Cafe Libero** (p81).

☀ Since you're in Dongmen, use an hour or two to explore the winding lanes of boutiques and curiosity shops. Don't forget to enjoy the enormous collection of cultural memorabilia in the **Formosa Vintage Museum Cafe** (p76). Avoid the long lines and opt for a late lunch at Taiwan's most famous restaurant, the dim sum palace of **Din Tai Fung** (p76).

☽ Head east as the sun sets west, checking out the one-stop gadget emporium of **Guanghua Digital Plaza** (p83) if you're in the mood for bagging some electronics. The **Zhongxiao Dunhua** area is prime real estate for boutique eateries. You'll be spoilt for choice. Try **Cha Cha Thé** (p81), a modern designer teahouse, or firm local favourite, **Yongkang Beef Noodles** (p77).

For a local's day of eating and drinking in Dongmen, see p72.

○ Local Life

Dining & Drinking in Dongmen (p72)

♥ Best of Taipei

Best Dining

Din Tai Fung (p76)

Yongkang Beef Noodles (p77)

Toasteria Cafe (p78)

Tonghua Night Market (p82)

NOMURA (p78)

Best Cafes & Teahouses

Water Moon Tea House (p80)

Costumice Cafe (p80)

Cha Cha Thé (p81)

Cafe Libero (p81)

Drop Coffee House (p82)

Getting There

Ⓜ **MRT** Da'an district is serviced largely by the red line from Dongmen across to Xinye Anhe and the brown line between Zhongxiao Fuxing and Liuzhangli.

Local Life
Dining & Drinks in Dongmen

Dongmen is an upmarket and cosy neighbourhood popular with both tourists and well-heeled locals that does food very, very well. At its fringes are some excellent izakaya (Japanese gastropubs) that are always lively. It's also a lovely place to stroll, with hidden parks, winding alleyways and surprising little shops and cafes.

① Begin with a Beer

Craft beer is all the rage in Taipei at the moment. Start the evening by joining local office staff just off work having a punchy glass of local brew. **Zhang Men** (19 Lane 4, Yongkang St; ⊙to midnight) has 16 of its own varieties on tap. The Mango Witbier (NT$150 for 200ml) is a light fruity number.

2 Old Prison Walls

It's just a five-minute walk west to the remains of the walls of the **Taipei Old Prison**. Built in 1904 by the Japanese, it was used to incarcerate political prisoners under Tokyo and again under the Chinese Nationalists. These moss-covered stone walls, cracked and leaning inwards, have a bleak air. Is that a ghost behind you or just a leaf blowing in the wind?

3 A Pause in a Park

Swing past the huge blue-roofed, white-spired church on Aiguo Rd and slip into a **tiny triangular park** on Lane 7, Lishui St. Rest on a bench and listen to the clatter of woks as families in the houses around you begin to cook dinner. There's a rock at the entrance, bizarrely, with a snatch of the lyrics from 'Starry, Starry Night' etched out in now faded letters. Can you find it?

4 Yilan Eats

When locals want authentic Taiwanese homestyle cooking they come here. **Lusang** (☎02 2351 3323; 12-5 Yongkang St; ⏰11.30am-2pm, 5-9pm; dishes NT$120-260) is a smart, narrow restaurant with a big picture menu on the wall. Choose a few of the Yilan dishes, its speciality. Don't fill up as there's more food to come.

5 'Ave an Avocado

You can't come to Taiwan without buying a drink, whether it be a tea, a juice or a milkshake, from one of the hole-in-the-wall stalls. To help digest your snacks from Lusang, order an avocado milk (NT$90) from **Bing Lifang** (⏰10.30am-10.30pm) on the corner. Avocados grown in Taiwan are larger with smoother skin than other examples, and some say they're not as tasty, but they still make a soothing and delicious drink.

6 Protest Park

Take your avocado milk to **Yongkang Park**. With its fringe of trees, slide and rides, and ample benches, this little patch of green is always full of playing children and retirees. There's a public toilet in the southwest corner, and a small bust of Chiang Kai-shek in the southeast corner. The park survived a plan to bulldoze it because local residents hustled up a protest. Grab a bench and enjoy this pocket of restfulness off busy Yongkang St.

7 Sake and Sayonara

Once rested, head back down Yongkang to Dongmen's best Japanese joint, **Tsubaki** (☎02 2358 7377; 46-1 Yongkang St; ⏰6pm-midnight). Squeeze onto a bench with all the happy Taipei people and enjoy glasses of chilled Japanese beer to wash down roasted butter scallops and platters of sashimi. In winter, the open-air pit-fire keeps your cheeks rosy.

Shandao Temple Ⓜ

Zhongxiao E Rd Section 4

Civic Blvd

Andong St

29 🔒

Qingdao E Rd

Linsen S Rd

Jinshan S Rd

Songjiang Rd

Jianguo Rd

Zhongxiao Xinsheng Ⓜ

Xuzhou Rd

Jinan Rd

ZHONGZHENG

Shaoxing S Rd

Hangzhou S Rd

Renai Rd

Renai Rd

26 🔒

National Concert Hall

Xinyi Rd

National Theatre

Chiang Kai-shek Memorial Hall

Formosa Vintage Museum Cafe

Dongmen

Xinsheng S Rd Lane 161

Roosevelt Rd

7 ⦿   2 ⦿   5 ✕ Xinyi Rd

← Yongkang St

Ⓜ

Da'an Park

Jinhua Elementary School

Yongkang Park

Aiguo E Rd

27 🔒

Lane 243 (Cafe Lane)

Qingtian St

Xinsheng S Rd

1 ⦿

Da'an Forest Park

Chaozhou St

Jinshan S Rd

Lishui St

Jinhua St

20 🔒

3 ⦿

Taipei Grand Mosque

Heping W Rd

Heping E Rd

13 ✕

16 🚌

National Taiwan Normal University (Shida) Lane 101

Shida Rd

Shida Night Market

Longquan St

Wenzhou St

Jianguo Rd

Roosevelt Rd

9 ⭐   23

Xinhai Rd

Shida Rd

14 ⦿

Xinsheng S Rd

Xindian River

Taipower Building Ⓜ

11 ✕

22 ✕

E

Lane 40

Andong St

Fuxing N Rd

Civic Blvd F

Lane 160
DINGHAO

Dunhua N Rd

⊗ 8

18 ⊗ Alley 223 G

Zhongxiao E Rd
Lane 248

Ⓜ
Zhongxiao
Fuxing

Da'an Rd

Ⓜ **Zhongxiao E Rd**

Alley 8
12 ⊗
Lane 280

6
⊗

21
⊕

Civic Blvd H

Guangfu S Rd

Taipei Dome
(under
construction)

Ⓜ **Sun Yat-Sen
Memorial Hall**

1

19 ⊕
Lane 219

28
⊕

Renai Rd

Renai
Traffic
Circle

Anhe Rd

Renai Rd

10
⊗

XINYI

Guangfu S Rd

2

Xinyi Rd Lane 147

Da'an
Ⓜ

Xinyi Rd

DA'AN

Dunhua S Rd

Xinyi
Anhe
Ⓜ

Xinyi Rd
Wenchang St

Keelung Rd

3

Fuxing S Rd

⊕ 15

Anhe Rd

Linjiang St

25 ⊕

Wild Bird
Society
of Taipei ⊙ 4

17 ⊕

Ⓜ **Technology
Building**

Heping E Rd

Dunhua S Rd

24
☆

4

Keelung Rd

National
Taiwan
University

For reviews see

⊙	Sights	p76
⊗	Eating	p76
⊕	Drinking	p79
☆	Entertainment	p82
⊕	Shopping	p82

Ⓝ

0 _____ 500 m
0 _____ 0.25 miles

5

Sights

Da'an Forest Park
PARK

1 Map p74, D3

This is Taipei's Central Park, where the city comes to play. And play it does, from kids rollerblading to teens shooting hoops and enjoying ultimate Frisbee to old men engaged in *xiàngqí* (Chinese chess). The park is a great place to hang out or to stroll about after a meal on nearby Yongkang St. It's also a great location for a picnic. (大安公園; Dàān Gōngyuán; Ⓜ Da'an Park)

Formosa Vintage Museum Cafe
MUSEUM

2 Map p74, C3

Documenting Taiwan's hybrid social and cultural history is this delightful private collection of Lin Yu-fang, a former dentist turned curator. Pieces range from Japanese-era commercial posters to shell figurines, musical instruments, temple implements and decorative carvings saved from the wrecking ball. The oldest piece hails from the Dutch occupation of Taiwan. It's a special experience to enjoy a coffee or tea at one of the old wooden tables. Entrance requires a drink purchase (NT$120). (秋惠文庫; Qiū Huì Wénkù; ✆02-2351 5723; 3rd fl, 178, Xinyi Rd, Sec 2; 信義路二段178號3樓; ⏰11am-7pm Tue-Sun; Ⓜ Dongmen)

Taipei Grand Mosque
MOSQUE

3 Map p74, C4

Built with money from the Saudi government and other Middle Eastern countries back in the 1950s, this modest, traditional structure is set in its own gardens; note the golden crescent moons topping the railings. Friday prayers attract a number of food vendors outside. Since this is a place of worship, tourists are advised to admire it from the outside. (台北清真寺; Táiběi Qīngzhēnsì; 62 Xinsheng S Rd, Sec 2; 新生南路二段62號; Ⓜ Da'an Park)

Wild Bird Society of Taipei
BIRDWATCHING

4 Map p74, E4

Dedicated to the protection of Taiwan's rare bird species, the society organises Sunday birdwatching trips in the city plus guided tours in Guandu Nature Park and Hua-Jhiang Waterfowl Park during the migration season. (台北市野鳥學會; Táiběi Shì Yěniǎo Xuéhuì; ✆02-2325 9190; www.wbst.org.tw; 3, Lane 160, Fuxing S Rd, Sec 2; 復興南路二段160巷3號; ⏰9am-9pm Mon-Fri; Ⓜ Technology Building)

Eating

Din Tai Fung
DUMPLING $$

5 Map p74, C3

Taipei's most celebrated Shanghai-style dumpling shop (the *New York Times* once called it one of the 10 best restaurants in the world) is now a

Taipei Grand Mosque

worldwide franchise. This is the place that started it all and daily meal-time line-ups attest to an enduring popularity. Try the classic *xiǎolóng bāo* (小籠包; steamed pork dumplings), done to perfection every time. Take exit 5 from Dongmen MRT. (鼎泰豐; Dīngtàifēng; ✆02-2321 8928; www.dintaifung.com.tw; 194 Xinyi Rd, Sec 2; 信義路二段194號; dishes NT$90-260; ⊗10am-9pm, ❄, Ⓜ Dongmen)

Ice Monster

DESSERTS $$

6 🍴 Map p74, G1

A popular shaved-ice joint with a wide menu of flavours, including strawberry, kiwi fruit and, most famously, mango. (✆02-8771 3263; www.ice-monster.com; 297 Zhongxiao E Rd, Sec 4; 忠孝東路四段297號; dishes NT$200-280; ⊗10.30am-11.30pm; ❄🛜; Ⓜ Sun Yat-sen Memorial Hall)

Yongkang Beef Noodles

NOODLES $$

7 🍴 Map p74, B3

Open since 1963, this is one of Taipei's top spots for beef noodles, especially of the *hóngshāo* (紅燒; red spicy broth) variety. Beef portions are generous and melt in your mouth. Other worthwhile dishes include steamed ribs. Expect line-ups at lunch and dinner. (永康牛肉麵; Yǒngkāng Niúròumiàn; ✆02-2351 1051; 17, Lane 31, Jinshan S Rd, Sec 2; 金山南路二段31巷17號; large/small beef noodles NT$180/200; ⊗11am-3pm & 4-9.30pm; ❄, Ⓜ Dongmen)

SHAHRUL AZMAN / SHUTTERSTOCK ©

Local Life

Home Cooking

When locals hanker for some home-style cooking they come to **Chi Fan Shi Tang** (喫飯食堂; Chīfàn Shítáng; 5, Lane 8, Yongkang St; 永康街8巷5號; dishes NT$180-300; ⏰11.30am-2pm & 5-9pm; 🚇; Ⓜ Dongmen). Chi Fan's dim lighting and grey slate and wood interior complement the modern approach, though the boisterous clientele keep the atmosphere down to earth. Try the cold chicken plate, the superb pumpkin and tofu (南瓜豆腐; nánguā dòufu) or the oysters in garlic sauce (蒜泥蚵; suànní hé).

Toasteria Cafe SANDWICHES $$

8 Map p74, F1

This very popular spot down a narrow alleyway has the best range of toasted sandwiches in Taipiei; from the classic grilled cheese on wholemeal toast to the Grapa (grilled smoked Gouda, red-wine onion jam, roasted garlic and fresh basil). Also doubles as a pub, with beer on tap and a cupboard full of cocktails. (📞02-2752 0033; www.toasteriacafe.com; 3, Lane 169, Dunhua S Rd, Sec 1; 敦化南路一段169巷3號; sandwiches NT$180-210; ⏰11am-3am Mon-Fri, 9am-3am Sat, to 1am Sun; ❄🚇; Ⓜ Zhongxiao Dunhua)

Beijing Lou PEKING DUCK $$$

9 Map p74, B5

One of the best Peking duck restaurants in town, with cosy old-school decor and attentive old-school waiters. The half duck is sufficient for two or three people. (北京樓; Běijīng Lóu; 📞02-2368 0058; 157 Roosevelt Rd, Sec 3; 羅斯福路三段157號; half duck NT$850, dishes NT$188-588; ⏰11am-2pm & 4.30-9pm; 🚇; Ⓜ Taipower Building)

NOMURA JAPANESE $$$

10 Map p74, G2

It's widely believed that, outside of Japan, Taipei is the best place in the world for Japanese food. Several Edomae-style sushi (sushi that follows the Tokyo traditions) restaurants have a great reputation for Michelin-level quality of food and presentation. Among these is NOMURA, named after the Japanese chef who founded the restaurant in 2011. (📞02-2755 6587; 4, Alley 19, Lane 300, Renai Rd, Sec 4; 仁愛路四段300巷19巷4號; lunch/dinner per person from NT$1500/3000; ⏰noon-2.30pm & 6pm-9.30pm Tue-Sun; ❄; Ⓜ Xinyi Anhe)

Sababa Pita Bar MIDDLE EASTERN $$

11 Map p74, C5

This Israeli-American venture has been serving delicious, healthy authentic Middle Eastern staples such as stuffed pittas and hummus for years now, and it never misses a beat. Inside, it feels like an Aladdin's Cave, and the experience is consistently good. Try the pita Beirut, with falafel and chicken. (www.sababapita.com; 17, Lane 283, Roosevelt Rd, Sec 3; 羅斯福路三段283巷17號; dishes NT$150-300; ⏰11.30am-9.30pm; ❄🚇; Ⓜ Taipower Building)

Slack Season Noodles

NOODLES $$

 12 Map p74, G2

An upmarket branch of a famous Tainan-based snack restaurant. Note: there's no English sign. Slack Season serves a long menu of southern dishes including mullet roe, bamboo shoots with pork, outrageously good fried shrimp rolls, and of course the noodles (a mere NT$50 per bowl). (度小月; Dù Xiǎo Yuè; ☏02-2773 1344; noodle1895.com; 12, Alley 8, Lane 216, Zhongxiao E Rd, Sec 4; 忠孝東路四段216巷8弄12號; dishes NT$180-420; ☉11.30am-9.30pm; ❄; Ⓜ Zhongxiao Dunhua)

Vegetarian Paradise

VEGETARIAN $

13 Map p74, C4

Because of its location (across from Shida University), this is usually the first vegetarian buffet many newly arrived students visit. The owners haven't let success go to their heads, though, and they still serve the same sublime vegetarian cuisine as always. Price is by weight. Note there's no English sign. (素食天地; Sùshí Tiāndì; 182 Heping E Rd; 和平東路182號; meals from NT$100; ☉11am-2pm & 5-8pm; ❄ 🍽; Ⓜ Guting)

Drinking

Something Ales

MICROBREWERY

14 Map p74, C5

Owner Arvin has more than 200 different types of bottled craft beer and usually one on tap – local and imported brews, Belgian and American IPAs. He keeps a low-key, comfy bar and might as well have a PhD in craft beerology. Note: the location

---

Understand
Understanding Taipei Addresses

Taipei is divided into 12 districts (區; qū), though most travellers will visit only a few. Major streets run east–west and north–south and are labelled as such (for example, Zhongshan North Rd). They are also numbered by section (Zhongshan N Rd, Sec 1) according to their distance from the city centre (basically where Zhongshan and Zhongxiao Rds intersect). When getting or giving addresses it's very important to know the street direction and section.

Taipei also has numbered 'lanes', which generally run perpendicular to the main streets. A typical address is 17, Lane 283, Roosevelt Rd, Sec 3. On Roosevelt Rd Sec 3, look for where number 283 would be. You'll find the lane instead of a building. The actual building address is 17 on this lane – in this case, the restaurant Sababa Pita Bar.

Then there are alleys, which are to lanes as lanes are to streets. It sounds complicated but after one or two tries it becomes intuitive.

will likely have changed in late 2016, but it's well worth seeking out. (195 Roosevelt Rd, Sec 3; 羅斯福路三段195號; 9pm-1am Sun-Thu, 8.30pm-2am Fri & Sat; Ⓜ Taipower Building)

Ounce Taipei

BAR

15 Ⓜ Map p74, F3

This slick speakeasy-style bar is everything you'd expect it to be: hidden behind a secret door, heavy on the dark hardwood and dim lights, and serving top-rated cocktails. The establishment is fronted by Relax cafe. On weekends, best get here before 9pm or you will struggle to snag a pew. (www.ouncetaipei.com; 40, Lane 63, Dunhua S Rd, Sec 2; 敦化南路二段63巷40號; ⏰7pm-2am Mon-Sat; 🛜; Ⓜ Xinyi Anhe)

Wistaria Tea House

TEAHOUSE

16 Ⓜ Map p74, D4

History, nostalgia and fine tea combine in this charming former Japanese-era wooden dormitory. Wistaria was built

in 1920 for naval personnel and later used as a hang-out for artists, literati and political dissidents following the 1979 Kaohsiung Incident (which led to the arrest and imprisonment of most of the top democracy advocates in Taiwan). (紫藤廬; Zǐténg Lú; ☎02-2363 7375; www.wistariateahouse.com; 1, Lane 16, Xinsheng Rd, Sec 3; 新生路三段16弄1號; ⏰10am-11pm; 🛜; Ⓜ Taipower Building)

Water Moon Tea House

TEAHOUSE

17 Ⓜ Map p74, E4

With some of the city's oldest and finest teas, an elegant design and classes in tea appreciation, this is the place for the serious tea drinker, or for someone looking to learn more about the art. Sundays see a large expat crowd of qigong enthusiasts. (水月草堂; Shuǐyuè Cǎotáng; ☎02-2702 8399; www.teawatermoon.com; 2, Alley 180, Fuxing S Rd, Sec 2; 復興南路二段180巷2號; ⏰2-10pm; 🛜; Ⓜ Technology Building)

Costumice Cafe

CAFE

18 Ⓜ Map p74, G1

This ultrahip cafe-bar has a marvellous leafy yard, perfect for a lazy afternoon wine or coffee. With draught craft beer and its semi-Gothic interior, Costumice is one of Taipei's most happening and welcoming drinking establishments. (☎02-2711 8086; http://costumice.com; 6, Alley 71, Lane 223, Zhongxiao E Rd, Sec 4; 忠孝東路四段223巷71弄6號; ⏰noon-midnight Sun-Thu, to 1am Fri & Sat; 🛜; Ⓜ Zhongxiao Dunhua)

Top Tip

Time for a Drink

A cold beer on a summer's evening at a roadside teppanyaki joint in Dongmen is a must-do drinking experience. Otherwise, Da'an has some of Taipei's best bars. For classy cocktails try the establishments around Xinye Anhe; for a pub experience or cheap preclubbing shots head to Zhongxiao Dunhua.

Da'an by night

Cha Cha Thé TEAHOUSE

19  Map p74, F2

Hyper-stylish but genuinely serene tea-house by designer Shiatzy Chen. One wall is made of compressed tea bricks. There's beautifully packaged tea for sale. (采采食茶; Cǎi Cǎi Shí Chá; ☑02-8773 1818; www.chachathe.com; 23, Lane 219, Fuxing S Rd, Sec 1; 復興南路一段219巷23號; ⏰11am-10pm; 🛜; Ⓜ Zhongxiao Fuxing)

Cafe Libero CAFE

20 Map p74, C3

Set in a house from the 1950s with vintage furniture and a Zelkovia parquet floor, this is the type of hip place you take someone to show them your insider knowledge of the city. Libero is on a street with another half a dozen excellent cafes. (☑02-2356 7129; 1, Lane 243, Jinhua St; 金華街243巷 1號; ⏰11am-midnight Mon-Sat, noon-6pm Sun; 🛜; Ⓜ Dongmen)

On Tap PUB

21 Map p74, G2

On Tap bills itself as 'Taipei's only real pub'; once you're inside you might indeed feel yourself transported back to a London pub. Big-screen sports, draught beer, hearty pub grub (pies and burgers and chips) and a lot of expats. NT$90 drinks before 8pm and a chilled beer garden make it a nice place for an evening tipple. (☑02 2741

5365; www.ontaptaipei.com; 21, Alley 11, Lane 216, Zhongxiao E Rd, Sec 4; 忠孝東路四段 216巷11弄21號; ⏰5pm-1am Mon-Fri, 11am-1am Sat & Sun; 🛜; Ⓜ Zhongxiao Dunhua)

Drop Coffee House
CAFE

22 Ⓗ Map p74, C5

Set in an 80-year-old gutted Japanese-era private residence with lovely worn wooden flooring. Serves single-origin coffee from places such as Rwanda and Brazil. The aroma of coffee hits you as you walk in. (滴咖啡; Dī Kāfēi; 📞02-2368 4222; 1, Lane 76, Xinsheng S Rd, Sec 3; 新生南路三段76巷1號; ⏰10am-11pm; 🛜; Ⓜ Gongguan)

Entertainment

Blue Note
JAZZ

23 ⭐ Map p74, B5

Taipei's longest-running jazz club, Blue Note has been in the same location since 1978. It's a moody little cavern in dark blue. Check its Facebook page (search for Blue Note 藍調) to see who's playing. Take exit 3 from Taipower Building MRT. (藍調; Lándiào; 📞02-2362 2333; 4th fl, 171 Roosevelt Rd, Sec 3; 羅斯福路三段171號4樓; ⏰8pm-1am; Ⓜ Taipower Building)

Bobwundaye
LIVE MUSIC

24 ⭐ Map p74, F4

This laid-back, foreign-run neighbourhood bar (the name means 'no problem') features regular live music, both local and international, and sees a similarly mixed crowd. See the website for events. Also serves hearty fried pub food. (無問題; Wú Wèntí; http://bobwundaye.blogspot.tw; 77 Heping E Rd, Sec 3; 和平東路三段77號; ⏰6pm-2am Mon-Sat; 🛜; Ⓜ Liuzhangli)

Shopping

Tonghua Night Market
MARKET

25 🔒 Map p74, G3

One of Taipei's liveliest night markets and all the better for being more local and less touristy. There's something for everyone. Food-wise there are steaks, sushi, animal-shaped biscuits, Thai, Vietnamese, candyfloss and the best rice-wine sweet dumplings in ice in the city. Shopping-wise there are lamps, jewellery, underwear, aprons, kitchenware, posters, puzzles and even a hippie shop selling Indian clothing and peace pipes. (通化夜市; Tōnghuà Yèshì; ⏰6pm-1am; Ⓜ Xinyi Anhe)

Jianguo Weekend Holiday Jade Market
MARKET

26 🔒 Map p74, D2

This giant market peddling jade and other semiprecious stones is under Jianguo Overpass. There are also beads, pearls, religious artefacts and copper teapots. Just south is a weekend flower market that smells heavenly and has some fine examples of bonsai bushes and orchids of many colours. (建國假日玉市; Jiànguó Jiàrì Yùshì; ⏰9am-6pm Sat & Sun; Ⓜ Da'an Park)

Zang Xi

BUDDHIST

27 🔒 Map p74, C3

There's no English name, but look for the colourful designs of Tibetan Buddhism and the Dalai Lama's portrait on the door. Inside is a treasure trove of Tibetan Buddhist paraphernalia, from shelves of mala beads, silver and amber jewellery to religious books and CDs. Look out for the stack of Tibetan language-learning magazines. (藏喜; Zángxǐ; 📞02-2322 5437; www.likecc.com.tw/; 23, Lane 41, Yongkang St; 永康街41巷23號; ⏰noon-9.30pm Tue-Sun; Ⓜ Dongmen)

Eslite

BOOKS

28 🔒 Map p74, F2

This is Taipei's most renowned bookshop chain, with locations all over town. There's a good selection of English books and magazines and it's worth it just to see all the Taiwanese reading quietly on steps, on the floor and in all the corners. (誠品; Chéngpǐn; 245 Dunhua S Rd, 敦化南路245號; ⏰24hr; 📶; Ⓜ Zhongxiao Dunhua)

Guanghua Digital Plaza

ELECTRONICS

29 🔒 Map p74, C1

Six storeys of electronics, software, hardware, laptops, peripherals, mobile phones and gadgets of all kinds. Dozens of smaller shops speckle the surrounding neighbourhood. You can likely bargain about 10% to 30% off the starting price; look uninterested. (光華數位新天地; Guānghuá Shùwèi Xīntiāndì; 8 Civic Blvd, Sec 3; 市民大道三段8號; ⏰10am-9pm; 📶; Ⓜ Zhongxiao Xinsheng)

Understand
All the Tea in Taiwan

Da'an has some of the nicest teahouses in the capital – Water Moon (p80) and Wistaria (p80), for example. Tea growing and drinking has a venerable tradition in Taiwan. While most people head to Maokong when they want to enjoy brewing and imbibing, there are a few excellent places within the city as well, many set in beautifully restored Japanese-era residences.

If **bubble tea** (*boba cha*) is your cuppa, good news: you'll find endless roadside stands and stalls throughout the city selling it hot or cold with ice. In Da'an, **Shida Night Market** (師大路夜市; Shīdà Lù Yèshì; ⏰4-11.30pm; Ⓜ Taipower Building) is a prime spot. Most of these places also offer fruit-flavoured teas, such as lemon or passion fruit, and sweetened or unsweetened black- and green-tea–flavoured drinks for between NT$30 and NT$60 a cup. Three of the most popular chains are 50 Lan, Comebuy and CoCo; you'll see them everywhere.

Note: if you can bring your own flask you can save on plastic and sometimes get a small discount.

Top Sights
Maokong Gondola

Getting There

Ⓜ **MRT** Take line 1 (brown) to Taipei Zoo station, then walk 500m south to Maokong gondola station.

Getting to the tea mountains at the southern tip of Taipei in Muzha District involves a vertiginous half-hour swing above the treetops in an eight-person gondola or cable car. Day or night, the views are stunning: the undulating treetop carpet below you and the city in the distance, at night, all twinkling with lights.

Don't Miss

A Ride in the Sky

A ride on the Maokong Gondola is inexpensive at NT$120 one way, and is an experience in itself. It's easily accessible from Taipei Zoo MRT station. There are three stops from the Maokong Gondola Station at the bottom of the hill just south of the zoo, one at the back of the zoo, one at Zhinan Temple and the terminal, Maokong Station. The gondola ride can be quite bumpy especially when it rounds a corner (at one point it turns almost 90°) and when it leaves from and arrives at a station. At certain points during the year, seasonal flowers can make the ride very beautiful: from January to February there will be white, pink and red apricot flowers, while April and May is the season for white Tung tree blossoms.

Crystal Cabins

If you have a head for heights, ask to ride in one of the crystal cabins called the Eyes of Maokong Gondola. The floor has been replaced with triple-layer reinforced glass.

Walking & Hiking

With its light traffic conditions, Maokong is a pleasant place just to stroll around on the roads. Turn left out of the gondola to head up the valley (it becomes delightfully remote in feel after 1km). Or head straight out along the main road and, after about 200m, look for a sign on the right that leads to a wide trail running through the tea fields along retaining walls. Maokong has a range of hiking routes that can be combined for full-day excursions. There are trail signs now in English and Chinese, so getting around is pretty safe.

貓空纜車; Māokōng Lǎnchē

☎ 02-2181 2345

http://english.gondola.taipei

one-way adult/child NT$120/50

🕙 9am-9pm Tue-Thu, to 10pm Fri, 8.30am-10pm Sat, 8.30am-9pm Sun

Ⓜ Zoo

☑ Top Tips

▸ On weekends the queues for the gondola can be mind-boggling. Come at 9am on a weekend or come on a weekday.

▸ The Gondola is closed on Mondays (although you can still get a bus up to Maokong – some teahouses will be open).

✗ Take a Break

Enjoy beautiful views and Chinese cuisine at **Yaoyue Teahouse** (6 Lane 40, Zhinan Rd, 🕙 24 hrs).

If you just want a coffee, head to the **Red Wood House** (31 Lane 38, Zhinan Rd, 🕙 10am-10pm).

Explore

Songshan

The big sights in Songshan (松山; Sōngshān) are all around the train station, home to the heaving Raohe Street Night Market, the clothing bargain bins of Wufenpu and the ostentatious Ciyou Temple. But the district also hides a local secret – south of the airport is Minsheng Community, a grid of tree-lined avenues of low-rise buildings dotted with parkland, funky cafes and designer shopping.

The Sights in a Day

☀ Start the day right with a hearty breakfast at **Woolloomoolo** (p93) before exploring the genteel neighborhood of **Minsheng Community** (p92), a world away from the rest of Taipei. Pop into **Fujin Tree 353** (p94) to pick up a map of the district. The imaginative works of local designers in several shops in this area make good photos and gift ideas.

☀ Head to the malls of Nanjing East Rd for lunch. There are the food courts in **Breeze Nanjing** (p97) and dim-sum dining at **Plum Blossom Room** (p94) – or, if you're craving Cambodian, **Ankor Wat Snacks** (p92) is a special experience.

☾ Reserve the evening for some real sightseeing. **Raohe Street Night Market** (p92; pictured left) is undoubtedly the big tourist draw here and is a great place to fill up on local goodies for dinner. At the eastern end of the market stands the ornate multilevel **Ciyou Temple** (p92) and a few blocks south are streets and streets of cheap clothes at **Wufenpu** (p97).

For a local's day in Songshan, see p88.

 Local Life

A Saunter Around Songshan (p88)

♥ **Best of Taipei**

Best Temples
Ciyou Temple (p92)

Best Shopping
Chuan-Der Buddhist Art (p97)

Wufenpu (p97)

Best Entertainment
Ambassador Theatre (p95)

Taipei Arena (p95)

Getting There

Ⓜ **MRT** All tourist sites in Songshan can be reached on the northeastern stretches of the brown or green lines. The key stations are Songshan Airport, Nanjing Fuxing and Songshan.

Local Life
A Saunter Around Songshan

Tucked away in Taipei's northeastern nook, Songshan sings to the beat of eager shoppers searching for Korean fashion bargains and evening snacking of beloved bites, both sweet and savoury. This energy and buzz feeds off a vibrant temple culture and a bridge over a light-shimmering river where local love is sworn.

① Temple Times

For locals, street temples aren't just for worship; they're part of life in a very non-religious way. Inside the web of Wufenpu market is **Jin An Gong** (peace-entering temple: ⊘5am-9.30pm). In the courtyard, with its gaudy scarlet pillars, there are ATMs, a noodle and tea stall with trestle tables set out next to the incense cauldron, and a small flying-dragon pagoda, where retirees sit, smoke and gossip.

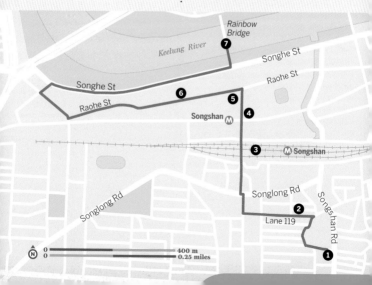

❷ Shopping for Sparkles

Taiwanese women, like moths to a flame, adore clothes and accessories that sparkle. See if you can find **Shēn Bǎi** (申柏; 25 Lane 119, Songshan Rd; ⏰3-10pm): the shop is stacked with sequined denim shorts, T-shirts and tops. There are knickers that glitter, caps with shiny studs, spangled belts and pink bejewelled bras that look like chandeliers.

❸ Japanese on Ice

Two of Taipei residents' favourite things, especially in summer, are air-conditioned shopping malls and Japanese food. Inside Citylink Songshan, above the Songshan Train Station, is **Tsujiri** (2nd fl; ⏰11am-10pm), an all-matcha tea and dessert shop from Tokyo, dating back more than 150 years. Try their best seller, the O-Matcha soft ice cream in a cone (NT$110): it's smooth and rich, and leaves the tongue with a tang.

❹ A Stop at a School

As you approach Ciyou Temple, can you smell chlorine and hear splashing? This public pool is part of the historical **Songshan Elementary School** (746 Bade Rd, Sec 4), built back in 1898. Walk around to the rear and peer through the railings: you should be able to see curious stone sculptures of lions with combed manes and giant seahorses, as well as cloisters framed with arches reminiscent of the Middle East.

❺ Night Market Nibbles

Enter the fray of **Raohe Street Night Market** (饒河街觀光夜市; Ráohéjiē Guānguāng Yèshì; Map p90, H4; ⏰5pm-midnight; Ⓜ Songshan) and queue for its most popular snack, the pork black pepper bun 胡椒餅 (*hújiāo bing*, NT$50 each) at the entrance; you'll know which stall, it has the outrageously longest line. One person pats the dough, another stuffs it with spring onion slivers, another with minced peppered pork, while another shapes it before baking. The end result is crispy, chewy and, of course, peppery.

❻ A Pair of Painted Shoes

Three-quarters of the way along Raohe's narrow spine you will find a spectacled lady busily painting canvas shoes with a tiny brush (NT$690 a pair, open 6pm to midnight). She dabs in colours or shades of grey; her designs include teddy bears, flowers, starry skies, meadows and rabbits or, for an extra fee, your own conception. She completes a pair in 40 minutes.

❼ Love Vows Under a Bridge

The **Keelung Riverside** is perfect for walking off Raohe's snack fest. You'll find sweaty joggers, schoolboys cycling, basketball in a net hanging from the handlebars, young boys strumming guitars, and teenage lovers canoodling on shadowed benches. Next to the **Rainbow Bridge** is a giant sculpture of the word LOVE. This is a designated love-lock site, where couples declare their passion by attaching a lock to the O, the V or the E.

Songshan
International
Airport

Minzu E Rd

Ⓜ Songshan
Airport

Zhonghan
Junior High
Ⓜ School
Minquan E Rd
Minsheng E Rd Lane 107

Minquan E Rd

10
🍴

Fuxing N Rd

Fujin St
7 🍴

Guangfu N Rd

Fujin St
🍴 1
SONGSHAN

Minsheng E Rd
13 🚇
Lane 6, Xinzhong St

Minsheng E Rd

Yanshou St

Xingan St

Qingcheng St

Dunhua N Rd

Changchun Rd
4 🍴
8 🍴

Changchun Rd

Jiankang Rd

Jiankang Rd

Nanjing
Fuxing
Ⓜ
9 🍴

12
🏛

18
🔒

Taipei
Arena
Ⓜ

Nanjing E Rd
Dunhua N Rd
Lane
81
11 🍴

15
✪

Nanjing E Rd

Fuxing N Rd

Fuxing S Rd
Bade Rd

14 ✪

Dunhua N Rd

Chang'an E Rd

Guangfu S Rd

2 👁

16 🔒

Civic Blvd

E   **F**   **G**   **H**

Minquan E Rd

Minquan E Rd

Ⓝ 0 ———————— 500 m
0 ———————— 0.25 miles

For reviews see	
◉ Sights	p92
✕ Eating	p92
🍷 Drinking	p94
★ Entertainment	p95
🛍 Shopping	p97

Keelung River

Sanmin Rd

Sanmin Rd

Yanshou St

Jiankang Rd

Nanjing Sanmin Ⓜ

Ⓢanmin Rd

Nanjing E Rd

Chang'an E Rd

Keelung Rd

6 ✕   Raohe St 5✕   3 ◉

Ⓜ Songshan Ⓜ

🔒17

XINYI

Yongji Rd

Sights

Minsheng Community
AREA

1 ◉ Map p90, D2

This is the place to watch Taiwan's hipsters while enjoying a street-side coffee or browsing upcycled designer wear. It's a secret little oasis from the traffic-choked streets full of shopping and towers. (民生社區; Mínshēng Shèqū; Ⓜ Songshan Airport)

Puppetry Art Centre of Taipei
MUSEUM

2 ◉ Map p90, D5

This small and fun museum (set aside about 40 minutes) showcases a medley of magical string, hand and shadow puppets, many with embroidered robes and fiery beards. The displays could do with a bit more English explanation but interesting snippets abound. String puppets, for example, were originally used more than 1000 years ago in exorcisms. (台北偶戲館; Táiběi Ôuxìguǎn; ☏02-2528 9553; www.pact.org.tw; 2nd fl, 99 Civic Blvd, Sec 5;民生大道五段99號2樓; ⏰10am-5pm Tue-Sun; ♿; Ⓜ Nanjing Sanmin)

Ciyou Temple
TAOIST TEMPLE

3 ◉ Map p90, H4

This 18th-century triple-tiered temple is dedicated to Matsu, the black-faced Chinese goddess of seafarers. It marks the start of the Raohe Street Night Market and is one of Taipei's busiest and most colourful temples. The rooftop *jiǎnniàn* (剪黏; mosaic-like decoration) is particularly vibrant. (慈祐宮; Cíyòu Gōng; next to exit X, Songshan MRT; ⏰6am-10pm; Ⓜ Songshan)

Eating

Ankor Wat Snacks
CAMBODIAN $

4 ✗ Map p90, A3

In recent years Taipei has seen the establishment of a number of tiny family-run restaurants serving excellent ethnic cuisine at rock-bottom prices. Ankor Wat is one of these. Try the *jiāomá jī* (椒麻雞; fried chicken on shredded cabbage) or Cambodian curry (東式咖哩; *jiǎnshì gālí*) with pho noodles (河粉; *héfěn*), rice noodles (米粉; *mǐfěn*) or French bread. There's a picture menu to help you decide. (吳哥窟小吃; Wú Gē Kū Xiǎochī; 454-2 Changchun Rd; 長春路454-2; dishes NT$85-100; ⏰11am-8.30pm Mon-Sat; Ⓜ Nanjing Fuxing)

Raohe Street Night Market
MARKET $

5 ✗ Map p90, H4

Taipei's oldest night market, Raohe St is a single pedestrian lane stretching between two ornate gates. In between you'll find a great assortment of Taiwanese eats, treats and sometimes even seats. Look for pork ribs in herbal broth, vermicelli and oysters, spicy stinky tofu and steamed buns. (饒河街觀光夜市; Ráohéjiē Guānguāng Yèshì; ⏰5pm-midnight; Ⓜ Songshan)

Display at Puppetry Art Centre of Taipei

Alla-Din Indian & Pakistani Kitchen

PAKISTANI $$

6 Map p90, G4

This curious canteen in Raohe Street Night Market (p89) is not that popular with the Chinese but it does pull in South Asian customers, which means, one, the taste must be authentic and, two, you'll probably find a seat. Food is served hot and spicy and in generous portions: big bowls of dhal, curries and greasy nan bread. This is not fine dining, but it's decent for the price. (阿拉丁; Ālādīng; 101 Raohe St; 饒河街101號; curries NT$180-200; ⏰5.30pm-midnight; ☑; Ⓜ Songshan)

Woolloomoolo

EUROPEAN $$

7 Map p90, B2

A perfect spot for a leisurely Sunday lunch melting into a boozy afternoon (there's wine and beer on the menu). Food is brunchy – avocado on toast and poached eggs – and is taken in a workshop-chic open-plan space. The name and the squat little bottles of Victoria Bitter at the bar give away the owner's Australian roots. (☎02-2546 8318; www.facebook.com/woolloomoolooTaipei; 95 Fujin St; 富錦街95號; meals from NT$200; ⏰10am-6pm Tue-Fri, 9am-6pm Sat & Sun; � ☑ ☑; Ⓜ Songshan Airport)

Jolly Brewery & Restaurant

THAI $$

8 Map p90, A3

Jolly, one of Taipei's few remaining brew pubs, does a roaring business nightly. The Qingcheng St branch has outdoor seating, while a new branch has just opened on Hengyang St, near Taipei Main Station in a historic building. Both serve good Thai food. (www.jollys.tw; 29 Qingcheng St; 慶城街29號; dishes NT$160-495; ⏱11.30am-2.30pm daily, 5.30-11pm Sun-Wed, 5.30pm-midnight Thu, 5.30-1am Fri & Sat; 🛜; Ⓜ Nanjing Fuxing)

Plum Blossom Room

DIM SUM $$$

9 Map p90, A4

Taipei restaurants rarely do dim sum well, with the exception of this classy (though loud and jovial, in the usual dim sum way) place in the Brother Hotel on the second floor. (梅花廳; Méihuā Tīng; www.brotherhotel.com.tw; 2nd fl, Brother Hotel, 255 Nanjing E Rd, Sec 3; dishes NT$220-350; ⏱9am-8.30pm; ❄; Ⓜ Nanjing Fuxing)

 Top Tip

Raohe Street Night Market

Loved by locals and tourists alike, Raohe Street Night Market (p92), which, unlike other night markets, is a long, single, narrow lane, gets jam-packed on weekends. It's infinitely more enjoyable and manageable on a week night.

Drinking

Fujin Tree 353

CAFE

10 Map p90, D2

With outdoor seating facing tree-lined Fujin St, this cafe is hard to beat. Inside it's all woodwork, mood lighting and strategically placed twigs. If you want to people-watch Taiwan's hip generation, this is ground control.

The Fujin Tree Group, which has also opened a designer housewares shop and a champagne and oyster bar, is responsible for driving this area's transformation into a trendy enclave. It has made a walking map of the Fujin St area, which you can pick up in the cafe. (☎02-2749 5225; www.facebook.com/fujintree353cafe; 353 Fujin St; 富錦街353號; ⏱9am-6.30pm Mon-Fri, to 7.30pm Sat & Sun; 🛜; Ⓜ Song-shan Airport)

Haritts

CAFE

11 Map p90, A4

This cute little Japanese cafe charms on two levels: it has a little flower garden where you can sip your brew to the sound of birds, and it offers no less than 16 different varieties of hand-baked doughnuts. Here are just few flavours to whet your appetite: Earl Grey, pumpkin and mango yoghurt. (☎02-8771 0645; www.haritts.com; 33, Lane 81, Fuxing N Rd, 復興北路81巷33號; ⏱11am-7pm Mon-Sat; 🛜 🐾; Ⓜ Nanjing Fuxing)

333

BAR

12 🚇 Map p90, A4

Blinged-out hotel bar with heavy drapes and minimal lighting – a creation of local designer Ray Chen. The big draw here is a healthy array of whiskies. A mini infinity pool behind the bar is mesmerising, especially after a few of those whiskies. (Hotel Quote, 333 Nanjing E Rd, Sec 3; 南京東路3段333號; ⏰11.30am-midnight Sun-Thu, to 2am Fri & Sat; 🛜; Ⓜ Taipei Arena)

Rokucyoumecafe

CAFE

13 🚇 Map p90, D2

This cute cafe is aiming to be a little bit of Tokyo in Taiwan, and hits very close to the mark. Its speciality is matcha, that favoured flavouring from Japan made from powdered green tea. Matcha lattes and home-cooked cakes are so green they look too special to eat. The coffee here is genuinely excellent and lovingly prepared. (六丁目; Liù Dīngmù; 📞02-2761 5510; 7, Lane 6, Xinzhong St; 新中街6巷7號; ⏰noon-9pm Sun-Thu, to 10pm Fri & Sat; 🛜 ♿; Ⓜ Nanjing Sanmin)

Entertainment

Ambassador Theatre

CINEMA

14 ⭐ Map p90, A5

This long-standing favourite is less busy than some, and offers a good mix of mainstream and alternative titles. The cinema is equipped with

D-Box (moving seats). (國賓影城; Guóbīn Yǐngchéng; 📞02-8772 1234; www.ambassador.com.tw; 39 Fuxing N Rd, Sec 1; 復興北路一段39號; tickets from NT$300; Ⓜ Zhongxiao Fuxing)

Taipei Arena

LIVE PERFORMANCE

15 ⭐ Map p90, B4

Vast, cavernous and shaped like a flying saucer, the Taipei Arena hosts concerts, and sporting and theatrical events. Some top international names have played here – Madonna performed at the arena in 2016. The attached Ice Land is a public ice-skating rink. (臺北小巨蛋; Táiběi Xiǎo Jùdàn; 📞02-2578 3536; english.arena.taipei; 2 Nanjing E Rd, Sec 4; 南京東路4短2號; ♿; Ⓜ Taipei Arena)

Understand

Asia's Slow Roast

Coffee Capital, Capital Coffee

The backbone of Mingsheng Community is the marvellous crop of cafes you will find here. You might be pleasantly surprised to see how much the Taiwanese have embraced the bean. The story of how this happened on an island whose traditional drink is surely tea is a bit of a mystery, but how and where you can get your hands on the perfect cup is not.

Bringing the Bean

It seems the Dutch first planted coffee around the Gukeng area (Yunlin County) in the 17th century, but for centuries the red beans were used only for decorative purposes by indigenous peoples.

Things really began about 10 years ago as Taiwanese living or studying abroad started bringing back new ideas about how to make proper coffee. Today you'll find scores of cafes serving gourmet coffee, often from single-origin beans (some locally grown), roasted on the premises and brewed in a slow, labour-intensive way right in front of you.

Coffee in Chinese

Americano – 美式咖啡, *Měishì kāfēi*
espresso – 濃縮咖啡, *nóngsuō kāfēi*
latte – 拿鐵, *ná tiě*
cappuccino – 卡布奇諾, *kǎbùjīnuò*
mocha – 摩卡, *mókǎ*

Add 熱 (*rè*) in front of drink name to mean hot, or 冰 (*bīng*) to mean iced.

Where to get a good cuppa

Passable fresh-brewed coffee is available at any convenience store for NT$30 to NT$50. Some of the best – and ridiculously cheap for the quality – coffee comes from chains like CAMA, which roast on the premises and cater to takeaway. And there are independent cafes all over the capital, from ones with street-side seating such as Fujian Tree 353 to cat cafes which offer the chance to cuddle a moggy with your mocha.

Shopping

Chuan-Der Buddhist Art
BUDDHIST

16 Map p90, D5

This stretch of Guangfu Rd has a gaggle of Buddhist shops, and this is mother of them all, with three floors of incense, statues, books, scrolls and beads. Most of the stock is Tibetan but there are Chinese Buddhist artefacts too. Even if you're not a believer, many of the items make beautiful gifts. Note the shop doesn't display its English name. (全德佛教事業機構; Quándé Fójiào Shìyè Jigòu; http://artevent.eslite.com/explore.html; 49 Guangfu S Rd; 光復南路49號; ⏰10am-9pm; Ⓜ Sun Yat-Sen Memorial Hall)

Wufenpu
MARKET

17 Map p90, H5

Wufenpu is a lively grid of streets, selling cheap clothes and accessories, wholesale and retail. You'll find big bags of T-shirts, jeans and shoes. It's an intense experience as the lanes are narrow and made more exciting by the snack carts and occasional zooming scooter (五分埔; Wǔfēnbù; off Songshan Rd; 松山路; ⏰11am-9pm Sun-Thu, to midnight Fri & Sat; Ⓜ Songshan)

Breeze Nanjing
SHOPPING CENTRE

18 Map p90, B4

Just across from Taipei Arena, this is one of the city's nicest shopping

malls: it's compact and a bit out of the way and so less crowded. It's filled with Japanese brands including Muji and Uniqlo; the Noodle Museum on the top floor has tasty bowls of udon and tempura; and there's a relaxed little coffee shop on the 2nd floor with good views. A great place to people-watch and get a taste of Taiwanese life. (微風南京; Wéifēng Nánjīng; www.breezecenter.com; 337 Nanjing E Rd, Sec 3; 南京東路三段337號; ⏰10am-10pm; 📶 👶; Ⓜ Taipei Arena)

Explore

Xinyi

Taipei's financial and city-government district, Xinyi (信義; Xìnyì) is the bright lights, big city part of town, with the tallest buildings (Taipei 101 of course!), the swankiest malls and the hottest nightclubs. And yet, nicely, it is also a green place, with hiking trails to Elephant Mountain and wide pavements circulating through the area where cyclists pedal along on city YouBikes.

The Sights in a Day

 If you're an early bird start hiking up **Elephant Mountain** (p106) around 7am and avoid the tourist hordes for some magnificent views of Taipei 101. It won't take more than half an hour at most to reach a viewpoint. Trip back downhill and if the skies are clear, zoom up to the observation deck of the tower itself for the view in reverse.

It's a 20-minute walk to **Sun Yat-sen Memorial Hall** (p105) from here, where the father of modern China is revered in a long, low traditional building with modern touches. Have a meat-free lunch at **Vege Creek** (p106) or a fish meal at **Supreme Salmon** (p107). Spend the afternoon soaking up the gorgeous grounds and renovated factories from the Japanese era at **Songshan Culture & Creative Park** (p105).

Have dinner in one of the many restaurants in the swanky malls, say **ATT4FUN** (p102) around **Taipei 101** (p100), and wind up the evening at **Frank** (p109) for some neon night-time views of 101, or perhaps you'd prefer some smoky, sexy jazz at **Brown Sugar** (p110).

For a local's day of shopping in Xinyi, see p102.

 Top Sights

Taipei 101 (p100)

 Local Life

Shop in Xinyi (p102)

💜 **Best of Taipei**

Best Entertainment
Brown Sugar Live & Restaurant (p110)

Best Bars
WOOBAR (p109)

Beer & Cheese Social House (p109)

Best Views
Taipei 101 (p100)

Elephant Mountain (p106)

Frank (p109)

Getting There

Ⓜ **MRT** Locations in Xinyi lie between eastern sections of the red line and the eastern sections of the blue line. Most sites are accessible from Taipei 101 (red), Sun Yat-sen Memorial Hall and Taipei City Hall (blue).

Top Sights
Taipei 101

This Taipei landmark has become synonymous with the capital. Throughout your stay you will probably gaze on this tower – which stands head and shoulders above all the other buildings in the city with its distinctive slimline bamboo silhouette – every day. You can whizz to the observation deck at the top for superior city views, but standing at its base or viewing it from afar is even more awe-inspiring.

台北101; Táiběi Yīlíngyī

⊙ Map p104, C4

☎ 02-8101 8800

www.taipei-101.com.tw

adult/child NT$500/450

⊗ 9am-10pm, last ticket sale 9.15pm

Ⓜ Taipei 101

Visiting

Ticket sales are on the 5th floor of the Taipei 101 Shopping Mall. The pressure-controlled lift up is quite a rush; at 1010m per minute it takes a mere 40 seconds to get from ground level to the 89th-floor observation deck. There's also an observation deck on the 88th floor, and an outdoor deck on the 91st floor is open on some occasions, weather permitting. Don't miss the massive gold-coloured iron wind damper that keeps the tower stable through typhoons and earthquakes. In the basement is a decent food court, and the first five floors are taken up by one of Taipei's swankiest malls.

Dining in the Clouds

If you don't want to spend NT$500 for a ticket to the observation deck, you can either book a 90-minute slot at the 35th-floor Starbucks (call 02-8101 8126 one day in advance; minimum charge NT$200) or book a dinner at one of the very pricey restaurants on the 85th and 86th floors. Ask at the information desk in the basement for their details.

Stability Ball

Hanging like a giant golden spaceship between the 87th and 92nd floors is the tower's 660-metric ton wind damper (that's the weight of more than 100 African elephants!), which visitors can view almost within touching distance. Its job is to stabilise the tower during strong winds; sitting in the path of summer typhoons, the capital is prone to some quite intense gusts. It essentially acts like a giant pendulum. You will only see it swinging during heavy winds – but it is impressive enough seen up close even when it's not windy, as these engineering secrets are usually kept hidden. It also helps protect the skyscraper during earthquakes.

☑ **Top Tips**

▶ To avoid the tourist crowds when visiting the observation deck, come just after opening (at 9am) or just before closing (at 9pm; note last entry is at 9.15pm).

▶ The best places from which to see Taipei 101 are the top of Elephant Mountain (p106), W Hotel's WOOBAR (p109), and Frank (p109) in ATT4FUN.

✗ **Take a Break**

The food court in the basement of Taipei 101 has Chinese, Thai, Taiwanese and Western food.

Pop over the road to Good Cho's (p107) for a Western-style lunch in a historic building.

Local Life
Shop in Xinyi

Taiwan tourism likes to say the capital's eastern district of Xinyi is Taipei's answer to Manhattan. While the comparison may be a tad optimistic, this upmarket forest of shopping malls, book-ended by Taipei 101 in the south and Taipei City Hall MRT in the north, is a fantastic place to people-watch, especially on the weekend, because this is where and when Taipei loves to play.

① **Studio Ghibli Shopping**

We start out in the most popular mall with young Taiwanese – **ATT4FUN** (Map p104, C3; www.att4fun.com.tw; 12 Songshou Rd; 松壽路12號; ⊘11am-10pm; MTaipei 101). In the basement you'll find the **Donguri Republic** store (11am-10pm) which sells official merchandise – stationery, plush toys and clothing – from Studio Ghibli cartoons (of *Spirited Away* fame). The queues for taking photos with a giant

Totoro and the bus-shaped cat from *My Neighbour Totoro* are usually long and squealy with kids.

❷ Time for Some Tea

Head up to the 5th floor for some tea. **Hanlin Tea House** (📞 02 7736 9918, 11am-10pm) is an extremely popular and elegant restaurant and tea brand. On the weekend it is usually packed with families. The company, originating from Tainan, is famous for its bubble tea (NT$70). It claims it invented the recipe, but it is not the only one to make that claim!

❸ Window Shopping

The air con is soothing in the summer, but head outside to the **pedestrian strip** (Lane 20, Songren Rd) to do some window-shopping and people-watching. There are plenty of benches and trees for shade and, although the shops are mostly international brands, it's all local at ground level. This stretch is quite lively with couples taking selfies, marketers giving out freebies and always a balloon seller or two. You'll also notice families taking out their elderly relatives in wheelchairs.

❹ Stopping for the Street Performers

Manhattan it may not be, but by midday the **street performers** have arrived, which gives it a bit of a Covent Garden feel. Families camp out on the floor to watch the acts, which range from acrobatics (balancing plates and juggling) to breakdancing youths.

('Gangnam Style' is almost always the background music of choice!).

❺ Getting Some Green

If you need a break from all that concrete, walk a couple of blocks west to **Zhongshan Park**, which fronts the Sun Yat-sen Memorial. This is a pocket of peace and is usually peopled with retirees practicing taichi, reading newspapers or just gossiping on a bench in front of the lake. Come evening, it's a popular place to fly kites.

❻ Lunching in Beijing

Just across the road is the strangely named **Beijing-Do It True** (506 Ren'ai Rd, Sec 4; 📞 02 2720 6417, 11am-2.20pm, 5-9.20pm) restaurant (look for the yellow sign). It began as a food stand in Kaohsiung in 1949, becoming a Taipei restaurant in 1969. Its claim to fame is that George Bush Senior dined here. The menu (English available) is traditional northern Chinese; try the sweet red jujube and white fungus soup.

❼ Finish off with a Film

The busiest section of Xinyi is the **Viewshow Cinema** (威秀影城; Wēixiù Yǐngchéng; Map p104, C3; www.vscinemas.com.tw; 20 Songshou Rd; 松壽路20號; tickets from NT$320; Ⓜ Taipei 101) building. There are 18 screens but it still seems as if that's not enough. The smell of popcorn is overpowering as you approach the building. Make sure you've got some warm clothing (the air con is brutal inside). Sit back and enjoy a film with the rest of Taipei.

Civic Blvd

Yongji Rd

Keelung Rd

Songshan Culture & Creative Park ◉1

Guangfu S Rd

6
⊗

Taipei Dome (under construction)

Zhongxiao E Rd

Taipei City Hall Ⓜ

For reviews see

◉ Top Sights	p100
◎ Sights	p105
⊗ Eating	p106
🍷 Drinking	p109
✪ Entertainment	p110
🛍 Shopping	p110

Ⓜ Sun Yat-sen Memorial Hall

8
⊗

3 ◎ Sun Yat-sen Memorial Hall

12 🍷

16 🛍

Zhongxiao E Rd

Songgao Rd

Zhongshan Park

Yixian Rd

Songgao Rd

10
⊗

XINYI

Renai Rd

Keelung Rd

Shifu Rd

Shizhi Rd

City Hall Ⓜ

Songren Rd

Guangfu S Rd

◎4 Discovery Centre of Taipei

✪ 13

Songshou Rd

15 🛍

14 ✪

Zhuangjing Rd

Taipei World Trade Centre

Shifu Rd

Taipei 101 ◉

Xinyi Rd

Xinyi Rd

9
⊗

Xiangshan Ⓜ

Ⓜ Taipei 101/ World Trade Center

Songqin St

Songzhi Rd

Songqin St

Songren Rd

Sungshan Nature Reserve

Village 44 ◎2

Guangfu S Rd

Keelung Rd

7
⊗

Wuxing St

5 ◎
Elephant Mountain

11 🍷

Sights

Songshan Culture & Creative Park

CULTURE PARK

1 Map p104, B1

Set in a former tobacco factory (or more accurately an industrial village) from the 1930s, this lovely park is part lush gardens, part frog-filled lake, part industrial chic, part workshop and part design studio. The place is dotted with pop-up creative shops, cafes and galleries. (松山文創園區; Sōngshān Wénchuàng Yuánqū; www.songshancultural park.org/en; Guangfu S Rd; 光復南路; admission free; ◯9am-6pm; ⓂSun Yat-sen Memorial Hall)

Village 44

VILLAGE

2 Map p104, B4

When the Nationalist army decamped to Taiwan in 1949, one million soldiers (and in time their families) had to be rehoused. Thus arose military dependants villages, which were once scattered across Taiwan. Village 44, in the shadow of Taipei 101, was Taipei's first. There isn't a lot to see here: a few old buildings and sometimes a photographic display in the main hall, but it is a pleasant parklike setting where you can sit and contemplate the tides of history. (信義公民會館; Xìnyì Gōngmín Huìguǎn; Xingyi Assembly Hall; cnr Zhuangjing & Songqin Sts; admission free; ⓂTaipei 101)

Sun Yat-sen Memorial Hall

CULTURAL CENTRE

3 Map p104, B2

The hall and its surrounding gardens occupy an entire city block. The latter are well used by picnickers, kite flyers, breakdancers and the early morning taichi crowd, while the cavernous interior serves as a cultural centre with regular exhibitions and performances. There's a large, though sparsely informative, museum on the life of Sun Yat-sen, the founder of modern China. The elaborate changing of the guards, with their extremely shiny boots, takes place every hour. (國父紀念館; Guófù Jìniànguǎn; www.yatsen.gov.tw/en; admission free; ◯9am-6pm; ⓂSun Yat-sen Memorial Hall)

Taiwan Design Museum

ARTS CENTRE

Housed in one wing of the atmospheric former tobacco factory (see 1 Map p104, B1), this exhibition space showcases modern designs. The ticket also includes admission to the adjoining Red Dot Museum, which focuses more on drawing. At the time of writing, ticket sales were a bit haphazard; tickets were being sold in Design Pin, a shop in the far western wing of the factory. (台灣設計館; Táiwǎn Shèjì Guǎn; www.tdm.org.tw; Songshan Culture & Creative Park; NT$150; ◯9.30am-5.30pm Tue-Sun; ⓂTaipei City Hall)

Discovery Centre of Taipei

MUSEUM

4 Map p104, C3

This is a great place to get your bearings on the city and its history. Maps and models show Taipei's evolution from a walled, gated city in 1882 to the bustling metropolis it is today. There are also exhibits, many interactive, on geography, topography, commerce, famous residents and natural resources. Use the western entrance to access the museum. (台北探索館; Táiběi Tànsuǒ Guǎn; www.discovery.taipei.gov.tw; 2-4 fl, Taipei City Hall; admission free; ⏱9am-5pm Tue-Sun; Ⓜ Taipei City Hall)

Elephant Mountain

HIKING

5 Map p104, D5

This mountain actually has its own MRT station (Xiangshan, which means Elephant Mountain). Just exit and follow the signs for about five minutes to the trailhead. Elephant Mountain is the vantage point of all the classic shots of Taipei 101, so expect a steep trail up. On weekends it gets crowded, especially around sunset. Don't forget to take water. (象山; Xiàngshān; Ⓜ Xiangshan)

Eating

Vege Creek

VEGAN $

6 Map p104, A2

One of Taipei's best vegan restaurants. The novelty here is that you choose the ingredients for a tongue-banging noodle broth – fill the plastic holdall with your choice of vegetables, fake meats, tofu, noodle type and tubes of fresh leafy goodness. Inexpensive, healthy and filling. There's another branch open all day in the basement food court of the Eslite shopping mall. (蔬河; Shū Hé; www.facebook.com/vegecreek; 2, Lane 129, Yanji St; 延吉街129巷2號; noodles about NT$180; ⏱noon-2pm & 5-9pm; ❄🌐🍴; Ⓜ Sun Yat-sen Memorial Hall)

Wuxing Street

MARKET $

7 Map p104, B5

In the shadow of Taipei 101 is this eating street and night market that arose to satisfy the tastes of mainlanders at nearby military Village 44. Look for steamed dumplings, beef noodles and pork rice, as well as teashops and modern cafes. The eating area

---

⦿ Local Life

Village 44

If the consumer crush of Xinyi gets too much for you, just cross over the road south to Village 44 (p105), where there's a nice grassy area to relax and a much more gentle vibe among the old houses. On weekends, this area is taken over by a small craft fair where you can buy cute gifts and be entertained by young performers singing and playing guitar.

ARIYAPHOL JIWALAK / SHUTTERSTOCK ©

View from Elephant Mountain

extends from Keelung Rd down to Songzhi Rd. (吳興街; Wúxìng Jiē; ⊙11am-9pm; Ⓜ Taipei 101)

Good Cho's
CAFE $$

Inside former military-dependant Village 44 (see 2 ◎ Map p104, B4) is this subdued cafe–performance space–lifestyle shop with marble floors, retro lighting and great acoustics. With its emphasis on history, community and local products, Good Cho's is a welcome break from the flash and consumerism of the Xinyi District. (好丘; Hǎo Qiū; 54 Songqin St; 松勤街54號; mains from NT$300; ⊙10am-8pm Mon-Fri, 9am-6.30pm Sat & Sun, closed 1st Mon of the month; ❋ ⋧; Ⓜ Taipei 101)

Supreme Salmon
SEAFOOD $$

8 ⍀ Map p104, A2

This bright, cheerful place has a dozen different ways to cook salmon – grilled, seared, braised, creamed in a pasta or sliced in a salad. All fish are sourced from Norway. For a taste of Taiwan, try the three-cup salmon with rice. (美威; Měi Wēi; ☎ 02 2731 1769; www.supremesalmon.com.tw; 320-2 Zhongxiao E Rd, Sec 4; 忠孝東路四段320-2號; mains NT$220-280; ⊙11am-9pm; ❋ ⋧; Ⓜ Sun Yat-sen Memorial Hall)

Chocoholic
FUSION $$

Everything on the menu at Chocoholic (see 1 ◎ Map p104, B1) has chocolate on

Understand

Breakfast, Lunch & Dinner

Most breakfast places open at about 6am and close by 11am or noon. A traditional breakfast in Taiwan usually consists of watery rice with seaweed (鹹粥; *xián zhōu*), clay-oven rolls (燒餅; *shāobǐng*) and steamed buns (饅頭; *mántóu*), served plain or with fillings. Other popular breakfast foods include rolled omelettes (蛋餅; *dàn bǐng*), egg sandwiches (雞蛋三明治; *jīdàn sānmíngzhì*) and turnip cakes (蘿蔔糕; *luóbo gāo*).

The Taiwanese generally eat lunch between 11.30am and 2pm, many taking their midday meal from any number of small eateries on the streets. *Zìzhù cāntīng* (自助餐廳; self-serve cafeterias) are a good option, offering plenty of meat and vegetable dishes to choose from.

Dinner in Taiwan is usually eaten from 5pm to 11pm, though some restaurants and food stalls stay open 24 hours (convenience stores are always open 24 hours).

The most important thing to remember in Taiwan when it comes to food is that some of the best things to eat are sold on the street – gourmands know that some of Asia's best street eats are found in night markets in and around Taiwan's cities.

it, in it or on the side, from a devilish dark-chocolate and rum fondue to the rather disturbing meat platters with grated chocolate. Located in the basement of the Eslite Spectrum shopping mall (p110). (巧克哈客; Qiǎokè Hākè; www.chocoholic.com.tw; Eslite Spectrum, Songshan Cultural & Creative Park; mains from NT$250-320; ⏱11am-10pm; ❋🛜🖊; Ⓜ Taipei City Hall)

Loving Hut

VEGAN $$

 ❾ ✖️ | Map p104, D4

One of the best branches of this vegan chain in Taipei. There's a choice of Western and Chinese dishes, and inventive use of very varied ingredients – for example, the house-special

risotto composed of plump brown rice in a sweet and tangy soup, with purple spinach, Chinese lettuce, carrots, tomatoes, apple slices, mushrooms, seaweed and squash, sprinkled with poppy seeds. (愛家國際餐飲; Àijiā Guójì Cānyǐn; 📞02-2346 0036; 247 Songde Rd; 松德路247號; mains NT$160-250; ⏱11.30am-2pm & 5-8.30pm Mon-Fri, 3-8pm Sat; ❋🖊; Ⓜ Xiangshan)

Bella Vita Gourmet Food Hall

FOOD HALL $$$

 ❿ ✖️ | Map p104, D2

In the basement of Taipei's most opulent European-styled mall, this gourmet food hall offers an oyster bar and patisserie, in addition to Japanese, Italian,

Thai, Chinese and more. If you go with friends, try the We Share Everything service: you order from separate venues and the food is delivered to your table in a special section. (www.bellavita.com.tw; 28 Songren Rd; 松仁路28號; ⏰11am-10pm; ❄️ 📶; Ⓜ️Taipei City Hall)

Drinking

Frank   BAR
This classy bar has a fantastic rooftop lounge with fake peach-blossom trees and glowing purple lamps, just one floor up from Club Myst in the ATT4FUN building (see 15 🔒 Map p104, C3). Taipei 101, lit like a firecracker, is directly above you. NT$500 minimum spend per person. (10th fl, ATT4FUN 12, Songshou Rd; 松壽路12號10樓; ⏰9pm-3am; 📶; Ⓜ️Taipei 101)

Beer & Cheese Social House   MICROBREWERY

11 🚇	Map p104, A5

Beer and Cheese is exactly that: dozens of very tasty craft beers paired with toasted cheese sandwiches or a cheese platter. The celebrity brew is the smoked snifter which is a solid beer poured over a chilled goblet of wood smoke. The place is itself is very 'man's club': dark walls, leatherette booths and a glare-lit bar area. (📞02-2737 1983; 117 Keelung Rd, Sec 2; 基隆路二段117號; ⏰6pm-1am; 📶; Ⓜ️Taipei 101)

Yue Yue   CAFE
This bookish cafe (see 1 ◎ Map p104, B1) with a piano, a sofa and green-shaded banker's lamps is open until 2am. The lattice windows, high roof and lazy vibe make this a marvellous choice for a late-night coffee or bottled beer. There's also seating facing the lake, but you may want to bring some mosquito repellent. (閱樂書店; Yuèlè Shūdiàn; Songshan Cultural & Creative Park; ⏰9am-2am; 📶; Ⓜ️Taipei City Hall)

Club Myst   CLUB
Pole dancers, an indoor waterfall and buckets of fancy booze; this is Club Myst in the aptly named ATT4FUN building (see 15 🔒 Map p104, C3). It has one of the capital's biggest dance floors and a swoon-inducing view of Taipei. (www.club-myst.com; 9th fl, ATT4FUN, 12 Songshou Rd; 松壽路12號9樓; ⏰10pm-4am; 📶; Ⓜ️Taipei 101)

WOOBAR   BAR

12 🚇	Map p104, C2

Inside the trendsetting W Hotel, WOOBAR is a quiet, natural-light–infused lounge in the day and a flashier neon-drenched nightspot after dark. It fronts the hotel's very special celebrity-graced swimming pool. (www.wtaipei.com; W Hotel, 10 Zhongxiao E Rd, Sec 5; 忠孝東路五段10号; ⏰10am-2am; 📶; Ⓜ️Taipei City Hall)

Entertainment

Brown Sugar
Live & Restaurant
JAZZ

13 ⭐ Map p104, D3

A bit hidden off Songren Rd is Taipei's pre-eminent club for R&B and jazz mixes. Brown Sugar hosts local house and guest musicians from around the world. Happy hour before 8pm and live music every day starting after 9pm. (黑糖餐廳; Hēitáng Cāntīng; ☏02-8780 1110; www.brownsugarlive.com; 101 Songren Rd; 松仁路101號; ☾6pm-2am; 🛜; Ⓜ Taipei 101)

Viewshow Cinemas
CINEMA

14 ⭐ Map p104, C3

This giant multiplex is always packed. Ticket prices are considerably higher than usual here, but with more than a dozen screens there should be something worth watching. (威秀影城; Wēixiù Yǐngchéng; www.vscinemas.com.tw; 20 Songshou Rd; 松壽路20號; tickets from NT$320; Ⓜ Taipei 101)

Shopping

Eslite Spectrum
MALL

Yes, there are lots of Eslite shopping malls around the city, but this one is special because it's set in the gorgeous grounds of Songshan Culture & Creative Park (see 1 ◉ Map p104, B1), it's full of independent brand stores, and there's a concert hall in the basement and a cinema showing independent films (tickets NT$270)! (誠品生活; Chéngpǐn Shēnghuó; http://artevent.eslite.com; Songshan Culture & Creative Park; tickets NT$270; ☾11am-10pm; Ⓜ Taipei City Hall)

ATT4FUN
MALL

15 🔒 Map p104, C3

This popular mall is good for kids, with the Donguri Republic store in the basement (selling merchandise from Studio Ghibli, of *Spirited Away* fame) and lots of cartoon-themed events. For the grown-ups there's also a swanky food mall, fashion brands, Club Myst (p109), the city's top nightclub, and Frank (p109), a ritzy rooftop bar. (www.att4fun.com.tw; 12 Songshou Rd; 松壽路12號; ☾11am-10pm; Ⓜ Taipei 101)

✓ Top Tip

Getting Around

Xinyi is easily walkable. It takes just 10 to 15 minutes on foot from from Taipei 101 to City Hall MRT along the pedestrianised strip. If it's baking hot, you can do most of this stretch inside the air-conditioned malls (they are linked by bridges). When you are hungry, just head to the basement where the food courts live. Alternatively hire a YouBike. The pavements here are broad and bike-friendly.

Songshan Culture & Creative Park (p105)

Eslite Xinyi

MALL

16  Map p104, C2

Spreading over two floors, the Eslite bookshop here (open 10am to midnight) is one of the best in the city, with teashops and a cute little cafe which, interestingly, also sells wine. There's a great food court in the basement with a fab juice bar,

and branches of the vegetarian buffet **Minder** (明德素食園; www.minder.com.tw; B1, Eslite Xinyi, 11 Songao Rd; 松高路11號; ⏱11am-9.20pm; 🍴; Ⓜ Taipei City Hall) and Supreme Salmon (p107). (誠品信義店, Chéngpǐn Xinyi Diàn; www.eslitecorp.com; 11 Songgao Rd; 松高路11號; ⏱11am-10pm; Ⓜ Taipei City Hall)

Explore

Shilin

Enjoying the fresh mountain air north of the Keelung River is Shilin (士林; Shìlín), an affluent residential area sitting at the base of Yangmingshan National Park. It's home to Taipei's best-known cultural attraction, the National Palace Museum (pictured above), and its most enduring night market.

The Sights in a Day

☀ Shilin doesn't really get started until noon, but if you get here early you can imbibe a decent coffee in **A Loving Cafe** (p122) and then take a leisurely stroll through the flower-filled gardens of Chiang Kai-shek's country retreat, the **Shilin Official Residence** (p119). By adding in a tour of the house you could easily spend an hour or two here.

☀ Go al fresco for lunch and dine at the marvellous **MiaCucina** (p121) for vegetarian, or there's **Din Tai Fung** (p121) in the basement of the SOGO mall. MiaCucina has wine if you're feeling a bit naughty. You'll need at least three hours for the next stretch – an immersion in Chinese imperial history at the **National Palace Museum** (p114). You could also take in the **Shung Ye Museum of Formosan Aborigines** (p119), across the street, if you have time.

☾ Your entire evening is for enjoying **Shilin Night Market** (p116), which is open until way past midnight. As well as the mountain of snacking to be done, you can explore the quirky **Cixian Temple** (p119), massage parlours, tattoo shops and funky little boutiques.

 Top Sights

National Palace Museum (p114)

Shilin Night Market (p116)

♥ **Best of Taipei**

Best History
National Palace Museum (p114)

Shung Ye Museum of Formosan Aborigines (p119)

Shilin Official Residence (p119)

Best Dining
MiaCucina (p121)

Din Tai Fung (p121)

Getting There

Ⓜ **MRT** Shilin is well served by the red line. Main stations are Jiantan, Shilin and Zhishan.

🚍 **Bus** Multiple routes go from outside Shilin MRT to the National Palace Museum.

Top Sights
National Palace Museum

The National Palace Museum in Taipei's northern district of Shilin is home to a marvellous and expansive collection of historic treasures. Numbering more than 600,000 artefacts, these are some of the most iconic examples of Chinese art and culture on public display.

故宮博物院; Gùgōng Bówùyuàn

👁Map p118, D3

221 Zhishan Rd, Sec 2; 至善路二段221號

NT$250

🕗8.30am-6.30pm Sun-Thu, to 9pm Fri & Sat

🚌R30

The Collection

The collection spans from painting, calligraphy, jade, ceramics, woodcraft and furniture to copper cauldrons. The recently opened Southern Branch in Jiayi County has meant that the two branches now share the collection. For example, in 2016, the famous jadeite cabbage was on loan from Taipei.

You will need a good few hours to really appreciate what's on display here – there are three floors, each with an east and west wing with themed exhibitions. There are always world-class temporary exhibitions as well as the (semi-) permanent collection on show.

Quake-proof?

Since Taiwan is prone to earthquakes, there is some concern that the artefacts in the museum could be damaged by a bad tremor. You will notice that many of the exhibits in their glass cases have nylon strings attached to them, as if they were puppets. This is to protect them in the event of a serious earthquake.

Visiting

Level 1 includes rare books, special exhibits, Qing and Ming dynasty furniture, and religious sculptures.

Level 2 includes painting, calligraphy, a history of Chinese ceramics and an interactive area.

Level 3 contains bronzes, weapons, ritual vessels, and Ming and Qing dynasty carvings. There is also the stunning jade collection.

The museum offers free guided tours in English at 10am and 3pm (book online). Alternatively, try an English headphone guide (NT$200).

To reach the museum from Shilin MRT station, head out exit 1 to Zhongzheng Rd and catch R30 (red 30), minibus 18 or 19, or bus 255, 304 or 815. It's about 15 minutes to the museum. From Dazhi MRT station take bus B13 (brown 13).

☑ **Top Tips**

As it's the top destination for all kinds of tourists, and especially massive tour groups, plan to visit the National Palace Museum when it opens late on Friday or Saturday evening. That way it will feel as if you have the museum to yourself!

✖ **Take a Break**

There's a nice coffee shop (open 9am to 6pm Sunday to Thursday, to 8.30pm Friday and Saturday) on the 1st floor.

For a proper Taiwanese dinner, grab a cab to Din Tai Fung (p121) in nearby Zhishan.

Top Sights
Shilin Night Market

Taipei's biggest, liveliest night market draws in crowds of both happy tourists and locals. By 8pm it's well and truly heaving. As well as all the sweet and savoury delights and games for kids, there's a warehouse-worth of T-shirts, flip-flops, jewellery, shoes, hats and toys. To top it all off, right at the heart of the action is an almost century-old Taoist temple.

士林夜市; Shìlín Yèshì

⊙ Map p118, C5

www.shilin-night-market. com

🕓 4pm-2am

Ⓜ Jiantan

History

Shilin Market started back in 1913 and gradually evolved into a night market. Over the past 15 years it's moved location for city planning reasons; the latest move was due to the construction of the fantastical and controversial Taipei Performing Arts Centre (p121).

Fun & Games

The lanes between Cixian Temple (p119) and the Shilin Market Building blast with techno music – this is where you will find all the games stalls. There's everything from simple handmade pinball machines, to shoot the balloon, to arcade games. Prizes are almost always stuffed toys.

There is also a lot of novelty fun in the snacks on offer. Shilin's specialities include oyster omelettes, shaved ice, lemon *aiyu* (jelly), penis-shaped waffles and ice lollies, and giant sponge loaves, which sometimes steam.

Temple Doors

Notice the doors of Cixian Temple: like many temples all over Taiwan, they are beautifully painted. In Taiwanese temples, painting is mainly applied to wood beams and walls. Though decorative, painting also helps to preserve wood, and is said to drive away evil, bless and inspire good deeds. Common motifs include stories from literature and history. Probably the most distinctive paintings at any temple are the guardians on the doors to the Front Hall.

☑ **Top Tips**

▶ Even though it's called Shilin Night Market, the closest MRT station is Jiantan (from Shilin MRT it's a confusing 10-minute walk).

▶ The market can get very crowded and claustrophobic. Try to come here just after 5pm if you want a bit more breathing space.

✗ **Take a Break**

To escape the crush and chill with a whisky or beer, head to Vagabond (p122) in Shilin.

There are foot massage places on Wenlin St, on the eastern margin of the night market.

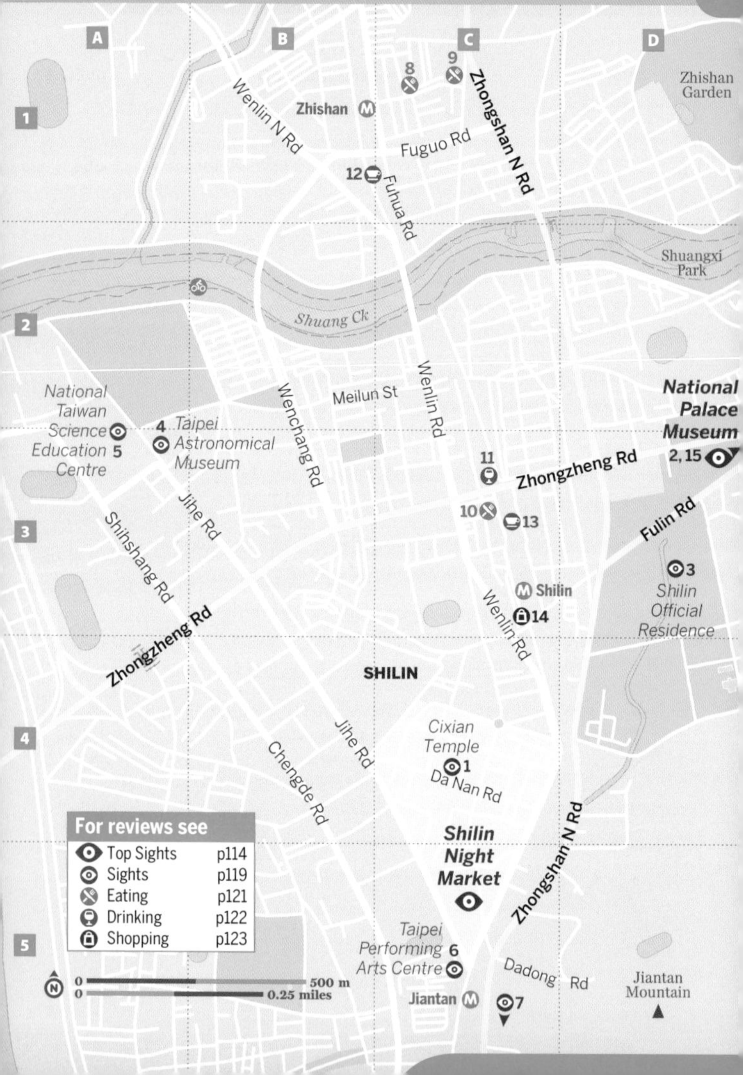

A

B

C

D

1

Zhishan
Garden

Wenlin N Rd

Zhishan Ⓜ

8
9

Zhongshan N Rd

Fuguo Rd

Fuhua Rd

12

Shuangxi
Park

2

Shuang Ck

National
Taiwan
Science
Education
Centre

4 Taipei
Astronomical
Museum

5

Wenchang Rd

Meilun St

Wenlin Rd

**National
Palace
Museum**

2, 15 ⊙

11

Zhongzheng Rd

Fulin Rd

3

Shihshang Rd

Jihe Rd

10

13

Ⓜ Shilin

14

⊙3
Shilin
Official
Residence

Zhongzheng Rd

Wenlin Rd

SHILIN

4

Jihe Rd

Chengde Rd

Cixian
Temple
⊙1
Da Nan Rd

Zhongshan N Rd

**Shilin
Night
Market**
⊙

For reviews see

⊙ Top Sights	p114
⊙ Sights	p119
⊗ Eating	p121
🍺 Drinking	p122
🔒 Shopping	p123

5

Ⓝ
0 _____ 500 m
0 _____ 0.25 miles

Taipei
Performing 6
Arts Centre ⊙

Jiantan Ⓜ ⊙7

Dadong Rd

Jiantan
Mountain ▲

Sights

Cixian Temple
TAOIST TEMPLE

1 Map p118, C4

Dedicated to the worship of Matsu, this 1927 reconstruction of the original 1864 design sits at ground central for Shilin Night Market. It's worth a visit (even if you aren't already in the area to snack) in order to examine the masterful cochin ceramic panels above the arched doors in the main hall, as well as the exquisite stone- and woodcarvings throughout. (慈誠宮; Cíchéng Gōng; 84 Da'nan Rd; 大南路84號; ⏰6am-10pm; Ⓜ Jiantan)

Shung Ye Museum of Formosan Aborigines
MUSEUM

2 Map p118, D3

There are currently 14 recognised indigenous tribes in Taiwan, and the exhibits at this private museum cover the belief systems, festivals, geographic divisions, agriculture and art of them all. Fine examples of tribal handicrafts can be seen on each level, and videos relate the tribes' histories and other aspects of tribal life. (順益台灣原住民博物館; Shùnyì Táiwān Yuánzhùmín Bówùguǎn; ☑02-2841 2611; www.museum.org.tw; 282 Zhishan Rd, Sec 2; 至善路二段282號; NT$150; ⏰9am-5pm Tue-Sun; Ⓜ Shilin)

Shilin Official Residence
GARDENS

3 Map p118, D3

For 26 years, this two-storey mansion and its elaborate Chinese- and Western-style gardens were part of the official residence of Chiang Kai-shek and his wife Soong Mei-ling. Today the entire estate is a lovely public park and even the house itself is open, though it merely displays the rather humdrum domestic life, and middle-brow tastes, of the Chiangs. The free audio guide is more than a little obsequious about the house's master and mistress. (士林官邸; Shílín Guāndǐ; 60 Fulin Rd; 福林路60號; gardens free, house NT$100; ⏰9.30am-noon & 1.30-5pm Tue-Sun; Ⓜ Shilin)

Taipei Astronomical Museum
MUSEUM

4 Map p118, A3

This children's museum houses four floors of constellations, ancient astronomy, space science and technology, telescopes and observatories. Though a good place to while away an hour, there is a dearth of English-language content. More English-friendly attractions (at an extra charge) are the IMAX and 3D theatres. The 'Cosmic Adventure', an amusement-park ride through 'outer space', was closed for refurbishment at the time of updating. (天文科學教育館; Tiānwén Kēxué Jiàoyùguǎn; www.tam.

gov.tw; 363 Jihe Rd; 基河路363號; adult/child NT$40/20, IMAX theatre NT$100/50; ⊙9am-5pm Tue-Fri & Sun, 9am-8pm Sat; P; MShilin)

National Taiwan Science Education Centre
MUSEUM

5 ◉ Map p118, A3

Interactive exhibits at this children's museum cover the gamut of scientific knowledge, from anatomy (a walk-through digestive tract!) to zoology (a cat's-head-shaped helmet that gives the wearer feline hearing powers) to chemistry, life science and physics. There are good English translations at every point. The 3D theatre (turbo ride and regular), sky cycling and special exhibits are not covered by the general admission ticket. (國立台灣科學教育中心; Guólì Táiwān Kēxué

Understand

The National Palace Museum: An Art Odyssey

The National Palace Museum (p114) traces its origins back thousands of years. As early as the Western Han Dynasty (206 BC–AD 9), emperors sent teams of servants to all corners of the empire to confiscate all manner of paintings, sculpture, calligraphy, bronzes and anything else of value. Many of these items eventually found a home in the Forbidden City in Beijing (established in the 1400s), a place that truly lived up to its name: unauthorised visitors could be executed.

With the Japanese invasion of Manchuria in 1931, the museum's contents were moved for safekeeping. The priceless treasures spent the war years shuttling across Chinese Nationalist Party (KMT) strongholds in southern China. Despite China suffering heavy bombing attacks for nearly a decade, virtually the entire collection survived and a public exhibition was held in Nanjing in 1947.

In 1949, near the end of the civil war between the KMT and the Chinese Communist Party (CCP), the collection was moved to the Taiwanese port of Keelung. When it became clear that a retaking of the Mainland was not imminent, plans were made to construct a new venue to showcase the artworks. In 1965 the National Palace Museum in Shilin was officially opened.

For decades Chinese leaders accused the Nationalists of stealing the country's treasures. These days, however, with Chinese tourists making up the bulk of daily visitors to the museum, such talk seems passé. More current is the challenge from the Taiwanese side: you can have your treasures back in exchange for recognising our independence.

Jiàoyù Zhōngxīn; http://en.ntsec.gov.tw; 189 Shishang Rd; 士商路189號; adult/child NT$100/70; ⊙9am-6pm Tue-Sun year-round, & Mon school holidays; P; MShilin)

Taipei Performing Arts Centre
ARTS CENTRE

6 ◉ Map p118, C5

This outlandish theatre complex designed by Dutch architectural firm OMA was still being built at the time of writing. It was scheduled to be finished by the end of 2016, and appears likely to be worth visiting if only to experience the suspended sphere-shaped section. (臺北藝術中心; Táiběi Yìshù Zhōngxīn; 60 Jihe Rd, 基河路60號; MJiantan)

Jiantan Mountain
HIKING

7 ◉ Map p118, C5

The mountain rises behind the Grand Hotel and has great views over the Keelung River basin and city. For access to the trailhead, cross Zhongshan N Rd from Jiantan MRT and take a short walk south. You can expect the main walking route to take about two hours start to finish. (劍潭山; Jiàntánshān; 🚌203, 218, 220, 260, 267)

Eating

MiaCucina
VEGETARIAN $$

8 Map p118, C1

Serving Italian food in American portions, this place is best enjoyed with a friend. Super popular, especially with expats; it's worth booking if you come at lunch or dinner peak times. Panini, fresh pasta, soups and salads – we recommend the sweet mustard panini with apple, caramelised onion, pecans, dried cranberries, mozzarella and sweet mustard. Mouth-watering! (📞02-8866 2658; 48 Dexing W Rd, 德行西路48號; mains NT$250-285, set meals NT$480; ⊙11am-10pm; ❄🏠; MZhishan)

Din Tai Fung
DUMPLING $$

9 Map p118, C1

This branch of the famous Din Tai Fung (p76) dumpling restaurant is a good opportunity to experience their legendary fare without the tourist crush, although you may still have to queue up. At least you can wait in the comfort of the air-conditioned SOGO mall. Good option if you're hungry after visiting the Palace Museum (p114). (鼎泰豐; Dǐngtàifēng; 📞02-2833 8900; www.dintaifung.com.tw/en; SOGO mall, B1, 77 Zhongshan N Rd, Sec 6; 中山北路六段77號; ⊙10.30am-9.30pm Mon-Fri, 10am-9.30pm Sat & Sun; MZhishan)

Vegetarian Kitchen
VEGETARIAN $

10 Map p118, C3

This friendly family-run vegetarian restaurant serves fresh and pretty tasty trays of meatless goodness – rice, noodles or cheesy pasta with vegetables, paired with a sweet lotus soup. There's lots of choice. (靜心健康素食坊; Jìngxīn Jiànkāng Sùshífāng; ☑02-8861 5141; 26 Meide St; 美德街26號; set meals NT$100-150; ☺11am-2.30pm & 4.30-8pm; ❀✦; Ⓜ️Shilin)

Local Life
Frappe with a Feline

Cafe Dogs & Cats is super popular with young couples or gaggles of girls, reportedly being the capital's first cat cafe and probably the cat cafe with the most cats – it is home to 14 cats and three dogs (including a shaggy golden retriever). The shelves are stacked with a menagerie of cat-themed knickknacks.

Feeding the cats with the cafe-sanctioned snacks will win you some minutes of frenzied feline friendship – or, if you're lucky, one will come and sleep in a basket next to you (there's one at every table). No children under 12 years old are allowed, and you'll get chased out or charged NT$100 if you just come in to gawp at the cats.

Drinking

Vagabond Cafe
BAR

11 Map p118, C3

This funky little arty cafe-slash-bar – not a bad whisky selection, by the way – has a youngish local vibe and a marvellous miscellany of furniture, from saggy old couches to study desks for laptopping. Wednesday and Saturday nights are movie nights. The entrance is on Lane 236, Zhongzheng Rd, directly opposite Shilin MRT exit 1. (流浪觀點咖啡館; Liúlàng Guāndiǎn Kāfēiguǎn; ☑02-2831 1195; 13 Fushou St; 福壽街13號; ☺noon-2am Wed-Sat, to midnight Mon; 🛜; Ⓜ️Shilin)

Cafe Dogs & Cats
CAFE

12 Map p118, B1

Cat cafes are very popular in Taiwan and this is reportedly the capital's first ever feline-filled coffee shop. Even though the staff aren't particularly friendly, it's a fun place for a creamy latte – they come with a cat-paw design in the foam that lasts right to the bottom of the cup. You can buy snacks for very many mostly sleepy cats. (小貓花園; Xiǎomāo Huāyuán; 129 Fuhua Rd; 復華路129號; ☺noon-10pm; 🛜🐾; Ⓜ️Zhishan)

A Loving Cafe
CAFE

13 Map p118, C3

Rather than queue up at the bland coffee chain round the corner, pop into this cute mellow cafe just behind exit 1 of the MRT. Single-origin coffee, lovingly prepared desserts and the

Eslite Bookstore

scrumptious-sounding Cointreau *rose au lait.* (愛上咖啡館; Àishàng Kāfēiguǎn; 📞02-2883 6180; www.facebook.com/aloving cafe; 47, Lane 235, Zhongzheng Rd, 中正路 235巷47號; ⏲noon-9pm Mon-Fri, 10am-6pm Sat & Sun; 🛜; Ⓜ Shilin)

Shopping

Eslite Bookstore BOOKS

14 🔒 Map p118, C3

A small branch of this popular chain, which stocks a selection of English books and magazines. Nice place to browse. Take exit 2 from Shilin MRT station. (誠品書店, Chéngpǐn Shūdiàn; 📞02-8861 1827; 340 Wenlin Rd; 文林路340 號; ⏲10am-10pm; Ⓜ Shilin)

National Palace Museum Shop GIFTS & SOUVENIRS

15 🔒 Map p118, D3

Gifts for all price ranges, based on the museum's collection (p114). There's everything from a tiny jade-cabbage phone pendant made from resin and costing NT$100 to a glorious round-bellied, Ming-replica vase in under-glaze blue with Indian lotus design for NT$26,800. (www.npmshops.com; B1, National Palace Museum; ⏲9am-7pm Sun-Thu, to 9.30pm Fri & Sat; 🛜; 🚌304)

Local Life
Riding up the River

Getting There

Ⓜ **MRT** Gongguan station, exit 1, drops you right outside the breakfast carts.

The blueish-brown Tamsui River wiggles its way up west Taipei, edged the entire way with broad bikeways. Taiwanese families in their thousands head here on the weekends for fishing, kiting, tennis, basketball, jogging and, of course, cycling. Safe from the city's crazy traffic, biking here is a lot of fun. The paths are mostly flat, so a YouBike is the perfect vehicle.

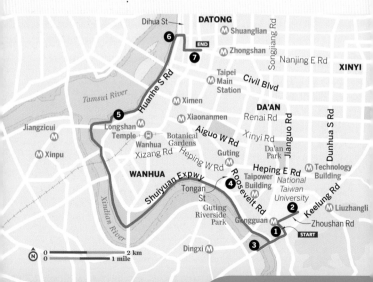

❶ Breakfast on Pancakes

Fuel up before the ride with a snack from the **breakfast carts** (Lane 90, Roosevelt Rd, Sec 4) next to the blue Wellspring Theatre building. Mrs Ding and her son have been selling pancakes (NT$30) here every day for six years (6am to 2pm). The savoury rolls come with slices of spring onion and crispy batter and options to add cheese or ham.

❷ YouBike the University

Cross Roosevelt Rd to the YouBike Station and cycle into the campus of **National Taiwan University**, scattered with historical buildings dating back 100 years. Head down Zhoushan Rd until you get to a large pond with a waterwheel: this is the university farm. A small **shop** (⏰9am-4.30pm, Wed & Fri-Sun) inside sells homegrown organic vegetables, tea and herbal medicine.

❸ Riffling through Junk

Cycle out of the campus the way you came and cross Fuhe Bridge. The sprawl of stalls underneath is **Fuhe Bridge Flea Market** (⏰7am-noon), which teems with bargain hunters on the weekend. Riffle through the buttons, typewriters, vintage fans, beaten up toys, shoes, cups, bags, ornaments, posters, and even rusty old power drills.

❹ Tea at a Bookshop

Cycle back over the river and down to the bikeway. At the end of Guting Riverside Park and the other side of the river wall is **Kishu An** (107 Tongan St; ⏰10am-5pm Tue-Sun; free), a beautifully restored wooden Japanese house that is now part bookshop, part teashop, part gallery and part history. You can explore the house as long as you take off your shoes and wear socks. Barefoot? Socks are sold for NT$20.

❺ Take a Break with the Birds

The bikeway meanders with the river, and you will pass mudflats and fields of reeds, as well as meadows and copses of trees. A good place to stop is **Huajiang Wild Duck Nature Park**, a popular resting stop for many migratory birds and Taiwanese bird enthusiasts waiting with their hi-tech photography gear.

❻ Arriving at the Wharf

When you arrive at the red-and-white ship sculpture, you're at **Dadaocheng Wharf**. On weekends, karaoke and live bands often perform here; it's a popular spot for locals to sit and soak up the river air. There are snacks and drinks stalls and this is also where you can access the city through the Water Gate.

❼ A Temple in the Air

Cycle through historic **Dihua St** (迪化街; Díhuà Jiē; Map p46, A8; Ⓜ Zhongshan, Daqiaotou) and onto Nanjing West Rd. Halfway up you will see a red-brick building with no windows and a tunnel at its base. This is Taipei's most bizarre temple, **Fazhu Gongmiao** (⏰6.30am-9pm). A road-widening project led to it being dismantled. It was rebuilt, elevated, in the 1990s. There are stairs up either side. When you're done, return your YouBike to the bike station a few blocks north at Taipei Circle.

The Best of
Taipei

Taiwan Lantern Festival (p144)
PHOTONCATCHER / SHUTTERSTOCK ©

Best Walks
Historical Taipei

🏃 The Walk

The tour begins in Wanhua, Taipei's oldest district, and winds its way around a selection of the wealth of well-preserved buildings from the Qing and Japanese eras that exist shoulder-to-shoulder with modern-day construction. The religious and educational sites are still used for their original purpose, while the others have been converted to fascinating museums, theatres and restaurants.

Start Longshan Temple

End Huashan 1914 Creative Park

Length 5km; four hours

🍴 Take a Break

In keeping with the historical theme, have a hot drink and light meal at the Mayor's Residence Art Salon (p36), one of the best-preserved wooden Japanese houses in Taiwan.

Longshan Temple (p63)

❶ Longshan Temple

Restored numerous times over the centuries, **Longshan** (p63) remains the spiritual heart of this district, just as it was when it was first established by Fujian immigrants in 1738.

❷ Bopiliao

One block east along Guangzhou St is this renovated lane that was a former bustling commercial area. **Bopiliao** (p65) has excellent examples of both late-Qing and Japanese-era shops.

❸ The Red House

Head north along Kunming St, turn onto Neijiang St and at No 25 turn left into the back of the **Red House** (p64), built in 1908 by the Japanese as Taipei's first public market. The area you are now in is called Ximending, a reference to the former west gate (*ximen*) of the Qing-era city walls.

❹ Zhongshan Hall

Now cross the road (note how the streets have widened) to **Zhongshan**

Hall (p63), built in 1936 at a time when architectural tastes were changing from Western classical hybrids to more modernist designs.

⑤ Land Bank Exhibition Hall

Follow Wuchang St east, turn right on Chongqing and then left again on Xiangyang. On your left is **Land Bank Exhibition Hall** (p30). Completed in 1933 and modernist in design, it still incorporated traditional arcades into the outer structure.

⑥ National Taiwan University Hospital

Cross the park to Changde St where, on your left, is the old wing of the **National Taiwan University Hospital**, built in 1912. The Japanese architect followed Renaissance style and at the time it was the most modern hospital in Southeast Asia.

⑦ College of Social Sciences National Taiwan University

Do a dog-leg onto Xuzhou Rd and cut through the **College of Social Sciences** along Shaoxing St. These buildings, completed in 1919, are a good example of how the Japanese often blended Eastern and Western elements: Grecian pillars and semicircular arches are topped with traditional Japanese black-tile roofs.

⑧ Huashan 1914 Creative Park

Cross over busy Zhongxiao East Rd to access **Huashan 1914 Creative Park** (p26), a restored wine factory from the 1920s.

Best Walks
Political Taipei

🏃 The Walk

Taiwan's modern history is a rollercoaster ride of authoritarian rule under the KMT, and the struggle for justice, democracy and Taiwanese identity. This walk is a journey that charts this turbulent and recent past; all sites are in Zhongzheng District, where the vast majority of political buildings, including the Taiwan High Court, are located. The walk is filled with irony, memory, controversy and hope, and it includes imposing architecture, a park and a broad boulevard.

Start Chiang Kai-shek Memorial Hall

End Legislative Yuan

Length 2.5 km; two hours

🍴 Take a Break

For a refreshing drink of traditional sour plum juice, pop into Lao Pai Gongyuan Hao (p37), on the west side of 2-28 Peace Memorial Park.

IMAGES BY KENNY / SHUTTERSTOCK ©

Protesters outside the Presidential Office Building (p30)

❶ Chiang Kai-shek Memorial Hall

We begin with the man who started it all and the landmark built to remember him. The **Chiang Kai-shek Memorial Hall** (p24) opened in 1980, five years to the day after the Generalissimo's death. His oddly smiling bronze statue gazes down at the vast square below, which was renamed Liberty Square in 2007 in remembrance of the Taiwan people's struggle for democracy against Chiang's then autocratic KMT Party.

❷ 2-28 Peace Memorial Park

Exit the square and walk up Zhongshan South Rd and onto Ketagalan Boulevard, passing the East Gate and the Taipei Guest House. Just on the right here is **2-28 Peace Memorial Park**, which marks the site of the 1947 uprising that was harshly put down by the ruling KMT. Inside the park there is a memorial and a small museum dedicated to the thousands of people who died.

❸ Ketagalan Boulevard

Emerge back out of the park on its southern side and look up the wide multilane **Ketagalan Boulevard**. Topped by the Presidential Office Building, in recent years it has been the favoured site for staging protests, the most notable being the 2014 march of the Sunflower Student movement, which attracted over 100,000 protesters demonstrating against the government's efforts to hurry through the passage of a controversial trade pact with China. Just imagine the street filled with that many people.

❹ Presidential Office Building

Walk to the end of the boulevard to get a closer look at the **Presidential Office Building** (p30). This handsome baroque-style structure, dating back to 1919, is where the president works even today. Note the armed guards standing out the front (it is possible to book online and tour the inside).

❺ Legislative Yuan

Swing back round past the 2-28 park and turn left onto Zhongshan North Rd. A few blocks north you will see the **Legislative Yuan** on your right. This is where Taiwan's parliament meets. The complex is a former high school for girls built during the Japanese era in 1927. In 2014 student protesters, as part of the Sunflower Movement, stormed and occupied the building for three weeks.

Best
History

Taipei has a rich story to tell from its past, with contributions from its indigenous peoples, Chinese immigrants and Japanese colonisers. The city has also used great care and skill in preserving, restoring and collecting this history, bringing to life the triumphs and the tragedies of its bygone years.

A Capital is Born

Before the 18th century, the Taipei basin was home to Ketagalan tribes. In 1709, settlers from China's Fujian province received permission from the Qing government to settle and develop Manka (present-day Wanhua). Manka and later Dadaocheng became trading centres for tea and camphor, fuelling economic development and further immigration.

When the port of Tamsui was forced open after the Second Opium War (1856–60), northern Taiwan began to surpass the south as the island's political and economic centre. Manka, the first part of the city to develop, grew rich with the trading of tea, coal and camphor.

In 1882 the city was walled in (the last Qing-era city to be so) and in 1886 it became the capital of the newly founded Taiwan province.

Japanese Efficiency

China ceded Taiwan to Japan under the Treaty of Shimonoseki in 1895 and Japanese troops entered Taipei that same year. Under Japanese rule the walls were torn down and a major redesign of roads and avenues took place. Taipei became the administrative headquarters for the colonial government, which developed railways, ports, city parks and public buildings such as museums. It also built infrastructure for Japanese workers, including temples and Shinto shrines.

JACK HONG / SHUTTERSTOCK ©

☑ Top Tips

▶ Most museums are closed on Mondays. The National Palace Museum is an exception.

▶ Many museums also provide free audio tours (use your passport as a deposit).

Best Museums

National Palace Museum The mother of all museums, home to thousands of exquisite pieces of Chinese art and historical treasures. (p114)

2-28 Memorial Museum The story of the terrible 28 February incident is told in this former Taiwan Radio Station building. (p30)

RICHIE CHAN / SHUTTERSTOCK ©

National Palace Museum (p114)

Taiyuan Asian Puppet Theatre Museum Full of puppets and puppet paraphernalia. (p56)

Shung Ye Museum of Formosan Aborigines Private space with excellent exhibits on religion, festivals and the supernatural. (p119)

Best Historic Buildings

Presidential Office Building The seat of power yesterday and today. (p30; pictured above left)

Lin Antai Historic House Beautifully preserved Qing-dynasty homestead. (p50)

Shilin Official Residence The estate of Taiwan's former dictator is surprisingly genteel. (p119)

Zhongshan Hall This palatial modernist-Western mansion is open to the public for free. (p63)

Best Heritage Areas

Dihua Street Preserved and crumbling 19th-century shophouses. (p44)

Bopiliao Restored alley of Qing and Japanese shops, popular as a film set. (p65)

Huashan 1914 Creative Park Japanese wine-making complex is made over into an artists' enclave and performance space. (p26)

Songshan Culture & Creative Park The long corridors of this converted factory have a wonderful institutional-throwback feel. (p105)

Worth a Trip

Take the red MRT line to the terminus station to find **Fort San Domingo** (红毛城; Hóngmáo Chéng; ☎02-2623 1001; 1, Lane 28, Zhongzheng Rd; 中正路28巷1號; NT$80; ◯9.30am-5pm Mon-Fri, to 6pm Sat & Sun, closed 1st Mon of each month; M Tamsui). Built by the Dutch in 1644, the main building housed the former British Consulate. The surrounding area has many fine examples of Chinese and colonial architecture, including Hobe Fort and Aletheia University.

Best
Dining

TOPPHOTOIMAGES / GETTY IMAGES ©

The Taiwanese love to eat out so much that many apartments don't even come with a kitchen. You've got local food at all budget levels – from big bowls of noodle soup to fine dining that requires reservations weeks in advance. There are all the Chinese cuisines, Southeast Asian flavours, and the Japanese legacy has given Taipei some of the best Japanese food outside of Tokyo.

Nocturnal Food Fun

One Taiwan experience you can't miss out on is eating at a night market. And Taipei's night markets are arguably the country's most famous.

So what kind of food can you expect to find on the fly in Taiwan? Some items won't surprise people used to eating Asian food back home. Taiwanese *shuǐjiǎo* (水餃; dumplings) are always a good bet, especially for those looking to fill up on the cheap. Stuffed with meat, spring onion and greens, *shuǐjiǎo* can be served by the bowl in a soup, and sometimes dry by weight. For a dipping sauce, locals mix chilli (辣椒; *làjiāo*), vinegar (醋; *cù*) and soy sauce (醬油; *jiàngyóu*) in a bowl according to taste. Other street snacks include *zhà dòufu* (炸豆腐; fried tofu), *lǔ dòufu* (滷豆腐; tofu soaked in soy sauce) and *kǎo fānshǔ* (烤番薯; baked sweet potatoes), which can be bought by weight.

Taiwan has its own menu of unusual tastes. While you're here you should try some of the local specialities.

☑ **Top Tip**

▶ The Taiwanese tend to eat an early dinner, around 6pm or 7pm (unless they are visiting a night market), and many restaurants tend to wind down by 9pm.

Dare to Try

Stinky tofu (臭豆腐; *chòu dòufu*) The classic Taiwanese snack.

Chocolate and meat Steaks and chicken breasts dressed with liquid chocolate sauce.

Iron eggs Braised and dried eggs with a black rubbery consistency.

Coffin cake (棺材板; *guāncái bǎn*) Deep-fried-in-egg toast planks, filled with a thick chowder of seafood and vegetables.

Stinky tofu

Pig intestines (薑絲炒大腸, *jiāng sī chǎo dàcháng*) Hakka-style stir-fried pig intestines with ginger.

Best Budget

Tonghua Night Market The best choice and the best prices, surrounded by locals. (p82)

Lao Shan Dong Homemade Noodles Fresh noodles, made in front of your nose. (p66)

Fuhang Soy Milk This Taiwanese breakfast place is so good the queue snakes down the stairs. (p34)

Best Fine Dining

Qing Tian Xia The delicate flavours of Guizhou. (p51)

RAW Creative French food designed by a celebrity chef; the hottest thing in Taipei right now. (p52)

NOMURA Japanese chef; intimate space. (p78)

Best Taiwanese

Yongkang Beef Noodles Going strong since 1963. (p77)

Din Tai Fung Taiwanese Michelin-starred dim sum. (p76)

Goose & Seafood Eat like a local on outdoor bamboo seating. (p52)

Best Japanese

NOMURA Japanese chef; intimate space. (p78)

Addiction Aquatic Development Mad market of Japanese everything. (p52)

Best Brunch

Woolloomooloo Aussie goodness and English-language newspapers. (p93)

Good Cho's Bagels and savoury pancakes. (p107)

Toasteria Cafe For that heavier – perhaps cheesier – plate of goodness. (p78)

Best Vegetarian

MiaCucina Western vegetarian dishes; almost heavenly. (p121)

Vege Creek Select your own ingredients for a yummy vegan noodle soup. (p106)

Best
Temples

Taiwanese clearly love their temples. And why not? In addition to being houses of worship, temples fill the role of art museum, community centre, business hall, marketplace, recreation centre, orphanage, pilgrim site, and even recruitment centre for criminal gangs and a front for money laundering.

NATTEE CHALERMTIRAGOOL / SHUTTERSTOCK ©

Architectural Features

The basic characteristic of any temple hall or building is a raised platform that forms the base for a wood post-and-beam frame. This frame is held together by interlocking pieces (no nails or glue are used) and supports a curved gabled roof with overhanging eaves. The layout of most temple complexes follows a similar pattern of alternating halls (front, main, rear) and courtyards, usually arranged on a north–south axis. Corridors or wings often flank the east and west sides, and sometimes the whole complex is surrounded by a wall, or fronted by a large gate called a *páilóu* (牌樓).

☑ **Top Tips**

▶ You can take pictures but try not to snap devotees without permission.

▶ Don't enter gated altar areas.

▶ Enter via the right door of a temple and exit via the left. The main door is reserved for the resident god.

Best Atmosphere

Ciyou Temple Triple-tiered blinged-out homage to the black-faced goddess of seafarers. (p92)

Longshan Temple One of Taipei's oldest and largest houses of worship. (p63)

Xiahai City God Temple Come here to pray for a lover. (p51)

Best Preserved

Bao'an Temple It won a Unesco award for its restoration and revival of temple rites. (p42)

Confucius Temple Gorgeously reconstructed with careful explanations. (p48; pictured above)

Best
For Free

You don't need tons of money to enjoy Taipei, and you can keep costs down by cycling a YouBike, eating from night markets and convenience stores and enjoying many of the free tourist sights listed below. Remember parks are free and if you bring your own water bottle you can fill up at MRT stations and many tourist sights.

HUANPHOTO / SHUTTERSTOCK ©

Best Tourist Sights

Presidential Office Building For admission, register online 72 hours beforehand and bring your passport. (p30)

Lin Antai Historic House Beautifully preserved Fujian-style homestead. (p50)

Botanical Gardens This leafy tropical hideaway is completely free. (p31)

Chiang Kai-shek Memorial Hall Includes an ogle at the smart soldiers taking part in the changing of the guard. (p24)

Best Entertainment

National Theatre & Concert Hall Free live jazz shows in the summer months are held in Liberty Sq between the halls. (p37)

Village 44 Weekend amateur music performances. (p105)

Xinyi The pedestrian strip between ATT4FUN and City Hall MRT is bustling with street performers on the weekends. (p102)

Best Museums

2-28 Memorial Museum Free on weekends. (p30)

Formosa Vintage Museum Cafe Entrance is free but you will need to purchase a drink to survey this massive collection of Japanese-era collectibles. (p76)

☑ Top Tips

▶ Joyously, temples are always free! However, donations are welcome, of course.

▶ While most museums and art galleries aren't free, ticket prices (except for the National Palace Museum) are usually around a token NT$30.

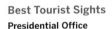

Best
Shopping

DINAH GARDNER / CUMULUS ©

With its endless markets, back-alley emporiums and glittering shopping malls, Taipei offers the complete gamut of shopping experiences. Go local and you can't go wrong. Taiwan has a rich tradition of wood, ceramic, metal and glass production and young designers are now pushing the envelope with everything from clothing to furniture. Taipei is also famous for its organic teas, dark sesame oil and pineapple cakes.

Souvenir Suggestions

Taipei gets creative when it comes to souvenirs; many tourist sites sell curious gifts such as tea bags with cartoon depictions of Chinese politicians, for example. Handicrafts are inspired by traditional Chinese arts and indigenous patterns. There's been a movement towards independent designers, Japanese-driven, crafting everything from kitchenware to hand-painted stationery. Reading is a national pastime; if you're looking for English material, Eslite (p83) is a chain bookstore that has branches across the country.

☑ **Top Tips**

▶ Bargaining is uncommon except in street markets, and even then discounts of just 10% are possible.

▶ Teashops often let you taste the tea before you buy.

▶ Support Made in Taiwan when you can – the country's ambiguous sovereignty status makes it difficult for it to make trade deals.

▶ Take your own bag; say no to plastic!

Market on Dihua Street (p44)

Best Gifts

National Cultural and Creative Gift Centre Government-sponsored shopping emporium selling good-quality, reasonably priced gifts. (p38)

National Palace Museum Shop Inventive use of replicas to make curious gift ideas, such as jadeite cabbage mouse mats. (p123)

Best Designers

Huashan 1914 Creative Park Young designers make cutesy or vintage-inspired products. (p26)

ArtYard67 Contemporary ceramics in a restored long shophouse. (p59)

Songshan Culture & Creative Park More globally influenced local designs in a former Japanese tobacco plant. (p105)

Best Traditional

Dihua Street Dried fruit, fish and herbs, and traditional crafts. (p44)

Lao Mian Cheng Lantern Shop Gracious handmade lanterns, with flowers, tassels, birds and other traditional designs. (p58)

Chuan-Der Buddhist Art A veritable hyper-market of incense, statues, books, scrolls and beads. (p97)

Best Markets

Yongle Market A forest of fabrics and tailors with their sewing machines ready to do your bidding. (p58)

Guanghua Digital Plaza Taipei's electronics market extraordinaire. (p83)

Wufenpu Piles of cheap clothing and accessories from South Korea, Taiwan and China. (p97)

Best
Entertainment

Taipei attracts a full calendar's worth of international performances and concerts, and also has its own home-grown talent to share. A number of venues specialise in traditional arts such as opera and puppet shows. The live-music scene is more happening than ever, with local and international bands playing in multiple genres nightly.

TWOSPEEDS / SHUTTERSTOCK©

Best Theatres

National Theatre & Concert Hall Fabulous and atmospheric, the capital's top venue for performances. (p37)

Taipei Eye High standard acrobatics and opera playing for the tourists. (p58)

Taiyuan Asian Puppet Theatre Museum Keeping the ancient art alive; irregular performances. (p56)

Best Live Music

Brown Sugar Live & Restaurant Sultry jazz and cocktails. (p110)

Riverside Live House Heritage building offering indie and rock shows. (p68)

Blue Note Taipei's longest-running jazz club still got the blues. (p82)

Taipei Arena International acts and mandopop stars. (p95)

Best Cinemas

SPOT – Taipei Film House Art-house movies in the former villa of the US ambassador. (p57)

Ambassador Theatre Less glitzy and more real; an old favourite. (p95)

☑ **Top Tip**

▶ **Taipei Travel** (www.taipeitravel. net/en) lists the dates for current and upcoming festivals and other large events; you can book tickets on **ArtsTicket** (www.artsticket. com.tw) and then pay at 7-Eleven ibon machines.

Best
Cafes &
Teahouses

One of the highlights of any stay in Taipei is a chance to soak up the atmosphere in one of the heritage-style teahouses and enjoy a fragrant cup of locally-grown leaves (from the Central Mountains). There are also thousands of independent cafes if coffee is more your thing; they are also a great place to connect to free wi-fi.

JUNG-PANG WU / GETTY IMAGES ©

Teahouse Culture

Drinking tea in Taiwan brings tranquillity, whether you opt to clink cups in a historic teahouse in a converted Japanese residence or take the gondola to the hills of Maokong for a rural twist. You can purchase tea sets fit for an emperor, along with fragrant packaged leaves from Taiwan's famous plantations, in many tea shops and teahouses.

☑ Top Tip

▶ Coffee chains are open seven days a week and tend to open earlier, around 8am, whereas independent establishments won't start business until 10am or noon.

Best for Chilling

Fujin Tree 353 Stylish street-side coffee house. (p94)

Cafe Dogs & Cats Creamy lattes with furry friends. (p122)

Costumice Cafe Hipster hangout with hidden garden. (p80)

Best Heritage

Cafe Libero Dark wood and parquet flooring in this refurbished house from the 1950s. (p81)

Yue Yue Lovely space next to a lake and a remodelled Japanese-era tobacco factory. (p109)

Dance Cafe Wistful wooden deck next to a Japanese-era dance studio. (p54)

Best Coffee

Fong Da Coffee Classic brews from the 1950s. (p67)

Drop Coffee House Single-origin coffee made to order. (p82)

Best Teahouses

Cha Cha Thé Designer drinking in Da'an. (p81)

Eighty-Eightea Enjoy a pot in the restored house of a Japanese priest. (p68)

Water Moon Tea House For the serious student of tea ceremonies. (p80)

Best
Bars

Taipei's bar scene has been growing more vibrant and diverse and there's now a nice selection of local-style bars, speakeasy cocktail lounges and expat-friendly beer-pulling pubs. The latest and most pleasing development is a new fashion for craft beer, many of them brewed here in Taiwan.

FUNKYFROGSTOCK / SHUTTERSTOCK©

Best Cocktails

Ounce Taipei Secret-door speakeasy. (p80)

WOOBAR Celebrity cocktails in the five-star W Hotel. (p109)

Red House Bar Street The best ginger mohitos in town. (p67)

Best for Beer

Something Ales Real craft beer without the pretentiousness. (p79)

Revolver Live-music joint with local craft brews. (p37)

Beer & Cheese Social House Speciality craft beers, smoky and chilled. (p109)

Best LGBTIQ

Red House Bar Street Al fresco, lively, camped-out family-friendly bar strip. (p67)

Goldfish Smart and stylish bear bar. (p54)

Taboo Raucous club for young lesbians. (p56)

☑ **Top Tip**

▶ Unlike eating out, which is very affordable, alcohol is expensive in Taipei. A beer will cost upwards of NT$150, mixers and cocktails will generally set you back at least NT$250.

Best
Views

Taipei is defined by its friendliness, its cleanliness and its liveability; as far as dramatic skylines go it's no Hong Kong or New York but there is, of course, the emblematic Taipei 101. Dig a little deeper and you will find some striking cityscapes that are begging to be photographed or simply enjoyed with a glass of something soothing.

Park Life

The serenity and gentle light of parks also make for great shots. Taipei is a gloriously green city: ancient trees, covered in vines and roots that mingle with paving slabs, create pockets of shade that are welcome in the summer heat. You will also stumble across mini parks, gardens and rich wooded hillsides all over the city, some with pagodas and pools of frogs, others with hiking trails and, occasionally, vegetable patches. While giant-sized Da'an Forest Park (p76) is the picnic choice for most, 2-28 Peace Memorial Park (p130) is a lovely central green space that offers a dignified reflection on a recent tragedy.

Best Views of Taipei 101

Elephant Mountain A gentle hike up this jungly hill affords tantalisingly close views. (p106; pictured above)

Frank The rooftop lounge is so close to the tower you could reach out and touch it with your fingertips. (p109)

Taipei 101 While you can't see it from the outside, the view from the observation deck of Taipei 101 itself will wow with its cloud-level vista. (p100)

Best Architecture

Chiang Kai-shek Memorial Hall Imposing, no matter which point in Liberty Sq you view it from. (p24)

Dihua Street Some shots straight out of history in this Qing-era shopping street. (p44)

Bao'an Temple A Unesco award winner for its exquisite woodcarving, painting and pottery, lovingly restored. (p42)

Best for Drama

Grand Hotel A palatial complex perched on Jiantan Mountain, visible from the overland red line MRT. (p147)

Miramar Entertainment Park Taipei's other skyline slogan, Miramar's Ferris Wheel looks best lit up at night. (p56)

Riverside As evening falls the city's lights shimmer in the river. A good spot is the Love Bridge. (p89)

Best
Festivals

Chinese New Year in Taipei is mostly a family event and many shops, restaurants and museums close during this period. The best Lantern Festival events happen outside the city. There are, however, dozens of vibrant, visually rich temple fairs each year, including those at Xiahai City God Temple, Qingshui Temple, Confucius Temple and Bao'an Temple; the latter has a two-month-long folk arts festival every spring.

PHOTONCATCHER / SHUTTERSTOCK ©

Best for Families

Taipei Children's Art Festival (Jul-Aug) Films, interactive exhibits, storytelling, puppetry, live theatre and more from local and international troupes and performers.

Dream Parade (Oct) Elaborate floats, stilt walkers, fire breathers, puppeteers, and dancers; a one-day Mardi Gras.

Best Religious

Baosheng Cultural Festival (Apr-May) Fireworks, folk theatre and dance in the magnificent Bao'an Temple.

Confucius Birthday (Sep) Solemn rituals in ancient dress at the Confucius Temple.

Night Patrol (Nov) Fabulous night-time three-day festival celebrates the resident god of Qingshan Temple.

Best Film Festivals

Urban Nomad Film Festival (May) Selection of local and international documentaries.

Taipei Film Festival (Jun-Jul) More than a month's worth of fantastic, often just-released, films from around the world.

Taipei Golden Horse Film Festival Internationally renowned, always featuring a great selection from Asian directors; Taiwan's Oscars.

Best Taiwanese Festivals

Taiwan Lantern Festival (Feb) Music, street performers, light shows and floating lanterns; this week-long event is held at the end of the Chinese New Year in Taipei Expo Park.

Taipei Dragon Boat Festival (Jun) Dragon-boat races are held at Dajia Riverside Park (pictured above).

Taiwan Pride Parade (Oct) Asia's biggest LGBTIQ street party.

☑ **Top Tip**

▶ For the dates of current and upcoming events visit Taipei City's website (www. taipeitravel.net) and the Taipei Cultural Centre website (www.tmseh.taipei. gov.tw).

Survival Guide

Survival Guide

Before You Go

When to Go

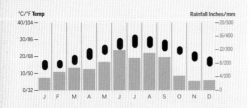

°C/°F **Temp**

40/104 —
30/86 —
20/68 —
10/50 —
0/32 —

J F M A M J J A S O N D

Rainfall Inches/mm

—20/500
—16/400
—12/300
—8/200
—4/100
—0

➡ **Spring** (late Apr–early June) and **autumn** (Sep–Nov) offer the best weather – neither roasting hot or miserably cold.

➡ You can see fireflies from April to May and enjoy tropical fruits from July to September.

Book Your Stay

➡ Taipei has a good selection of accommodation for all budgets. The most densely serviced areas are around Taipei Main Station, Ximen and Zhongshan MRT stations.

➡ The biggest discounts are always offered online and to those who book at least a month ahead.

➡ Many hostels are technically illegal due to antiquated regulations; they might not have signs outside and may not be open to drop-ins. Booking online is best. Note that an unlicensed hostel does not necessarily meet the government's safety standards.

Useful Websites

Travel.Taipei (www.taipeitravel.net/en) Taipei government website with hotel listings.

Lonely Planet (lonelyplanet.com/taiwan/taipei/

hotels) Recommendations and bookings.

Best Budget

Banana Hostel (www. facebook.com/Banana Hostel) Taipei's friendliest hostel. Bonus: free bananas! Close to Dong-men MRT.

three little birds (www. threelittlebirdstpe.com) LGBT-run hostel in Da'an, friendly to everyone.

Flip Flop Hostel (www. flipflophostel.com) Bunks in an atmospheric former railway-workers' dormitory. Just north of Taipei Main Station.

Sleepy Dragon Hostel (www.sleepydragonhostel. com) Family-run dorms, a chopstick's throw from Raohe Street Night Market.

Best Midrange

Attic (attic.artistvillage. org/en) Riverside artists' retreat near Gongguan MRT.

Jianshan Hotel (jian shan1977.com) Vintage nook right next to lovely Dihua St.

Simple Hotel (www. simplehotel.com.tw) Midrange residence with

understated style near Nanjing Fuxing MRT.

Rido Waikoloa Hotel (www.rido.com.tw) Quirky charm on Da'an Forest Park's northern fringe.

Best Top End

W Hotel (www.wtaipei. com) Iconic five-star near City Hall, with the potential for celebrity sightings.

Eslite Hotel (www. eslitehotel.com) Taipei's most tasteful five-star hotel located in beautiful Songshan Park.

Grand Hotel (www. grand-hotel.org) Live like an emperor up on the hill in Shilin.

Mandarin Oriental Taipei (www.manda rinoriental.com/taipei) Opulence on a sleepy boulevard near Song-shan Airport.

Arriving in Taipei

From Taoyuan Airport

This international airport (www.taoyuan-airport. com) is about 40km west

of the city in Hsinchu County and has two terminals (a third will be ready by 2020).

Bus There are half a dozen buses (NT$115-NT$150, leaving every 20 to 30 minutes) to various locations across Taipei. Average journey time is 50 to 90 minutes, depending on traffic and end point.

High Speed Rail To take the high speed rail you will first have to take a 20-minute bus trip (NT$30) to Taoyuan HSR station and then catch a northbound train (NT$160, 19 minutes to Taipei Main Station).

MRT A link between downtown Taipei and the airport is scheduled to open in the first half of 2017.

Taxi Taxi trips take about 45 minutes to an hour (fare around NT$1200).

From Songshan Airport

This smaller airport (www.tsa.gov.tw/tsa/en/ home.aspx) is just north of the city centre and services direct international flights to China, Japan and South Korea, plus domestic routes.

MRT When you arrive, you are already in downtown Taipei and connected to the rest of the city by the Songshan AIrport MRT station on the brown line.

Taxi There's a taxi rank outside the airport.

Getting Around

MRT (Taipei Metro)

➡ Clean and safe, MRT trains run from 6am until midnight.

➡ Most places in the city centre are within a 20-minute walk of a station.

➡ Announcements and signs are in Chinese and English, as are fares and routes at ticket machines.

➡ Coins and bills are accepted and change is provided, though it's best to buy day passes or an EasyCard.

➡ All stations have clean public toilets which you can use even if you are not riding the MRT (just ask the booth attendant to let you in).

➡ There are five lines: line 1 is brown, line 2 red, line 3 green, line 4 orange, and line 5 is blue. Both the brown and red lines have stretches that go above ground. Line 1 is a driverless train, so try to head to the front or back carriages for the best view.

➡ Fares depend on length of journey and vary from NT$20 to NT$65.

Bus

➡ City buses are generally clean and comfortable and run frequently.

➡ A useful app showing bus arrivals is 'Bus-Tracker Taipei' but it's in Chinese only.

➡ Fares are NT$15 on most short routes within the city centre. If the sign over the fare box reads 上車 (*shàngchē*), that means you pay when getting on, while 下車 (*xiàchē*) means you pay when getting off. The easiest way is to swipe your EasyCard, although coins are also accepted.

➡ Bus service times vary according to the route –

Tickets & Passes

If you are going to do a fair amount of travel by public transport it would be worth your while getting one of the two passes below.

➡ The more useful of the two, the **EasyCard**, is a stored-value card which can be bought in most MRT stations for a returnable deposit of NT$100. They can be used on the MRT, buses, some local trains, nonreserved high speed rail (HSR) rides, some taxis, the YouBike program and for purchases at all convenience stores, Starbucks, and dozens of other shops. Add value to the card at any MRT station or 7-Eleven.

➡ The **TaipeiPass** is a card that offers unlimited travel on the MRT and bus services in the city. Buy it at any MRT station. Cards are valid for one day (NT$180), two days (NT$310), three days (NT$440) or five days (NT$700). The TaipeiPass only makes sense if you are making many long journeys on the MRT.

most run from roughly 5am to around 11pm.

➡ Route maps shown at bus stops are only in Chinese.

Taxi

➡ The flagfall is NT$70 for the first 1.25km plus NT$5 for each 200m thereafter. From 11pm to 6am there is a surcharge of NT$20 on top of the fare.

➡ You can find yellow cabs all over the city and at all hours, but drivers may not be able to speak much English.

➡ Call the taxi hotline on ☏0800-055 850 (wait for the message and press 2; on a mobile phone call ☏55850). Call ☏02-2799 7997 for English-speaking drivers.

YouBike

➡ The city's excellent YouBike (taipei.youbike. com.tw/en) shared-bicycle program offers thousands of bikes at more than 150 stations. Bikes can be hired at one location and dropped off at another. Each 30 minutes costs NT$10 (after four hours the price goes up). You will need an EasyCard (register the card on the YouBike

website and you'll need access to a phone to accept a code sent by SMS) or a credit card.

➡ Taipei is mostly flat and almost all major roads now have wide pavements that can be ridden upon. There are also hundreds of kilometres of riverside paths.

➡ Most YouBike stations are outside MRT stations and near major tourist sites. The smartphone app 'Fun Travel in Taipei' shows the location of all stations, or you can consult the YouBike website.

Essential Information

Business Hours

Some restaurants and cafes and many museums are closed on Mondays. Bars and some restaurants often stay open an hour or so later on Fridays and Saturdays.

Banks 9am–3.30pm Monday to Friday

Cafes noon-8pm (often closed on Monday)

Museums 9am–5pm Tuesday to Sunday

Night markets 6pm–midnight

Post offices 8am–5pm Monday to Friday; larger offices may open till 9pm and have limited hours on weekends

Restaurants 11.30am–2pm and 5–9pm

Shops 10am–9pm, department stores 11am–9.30pm, supermarkets to at least 8pm, sometimes 24 hours; convenience stores 24 hours

Discounts

➡ Children's discounts are available and are based on height (rules vary, from 90cm to 150cm) or age (usually under 12). Foreign children are usually eligible for this discount.

➡ Seniors 65 years and older are usually given the same discounts as children. Seniors over 70 often get in free. Foreign seniors are usually eligible for this discount.

➡ Pop into a Taipei Visitor Information Centre: many of their maps and leaflets have coupons for small discounts at tourist-oriented shops and restaurants.

Electricity

110V/60Hz

110V/60Hz

Money

➡ Taiwan's currency is the New Taiwanese Dollar (NT$); you won't be able to use other currencies in Taipei.

➡ When changing money the best rates are given by banks. Not all banks will change money and some will only change US dollars. The best options for other currencies are Mega Bank and the Bank of Taiwan, or money changers at the airport.

➡ Apart from at the airport, there are few private money changers in Taiwan and there is no black market.

ATMs

➡ ATMs are widely available at banks, convenience stores, post offices and MRT stations, and most are linked with Visa, MasterCard, JCB, Plus, Cirrus and American Express.

➡ There may be limits on the amount of cash you can withdraw per transaction or per day (often NT$20,000 or NT$30,000).

Credit Cards

➡ Credit cards are widely accepted in midange and top-end restaurants, hotels and shops.

➡ Many budget hotels, most hostels, and stalls and night-market food joints never take credit cards.

Public Holidays

Founding Day/New Year's Day 1 January

Chinese Lunar New Year January or February, usually four to nine days

Peace Memorial Day 2-28 Day; 28 February

Tomb Sweeping Day 5 April

Labour Day 1 May

Dragon Boat Festival 5th day of the 5th lunar month; usually in June

Emergencies & Important Numbers

24-hour toll-free travel information hotline
☏ 0800-011765

English-language directory assistance ☏ 106

Fire & ambulance ☏ 119

Police ☏ 110

Mid-Autumn Festival
5th day of the 8th lunar month; usually September

National Day 10 October

Toilets

➜ Taipei is flush with clean, free public toilets. You'll find them in parks, transport stations (including MRT stations), shopping malls, public offices, museums, temples and rest areas.

➜ While most public toilets are squat style, there are usually at least one or two stalls with Western-style sit-down toilets. Public toilets often also have toilet paper.

➜ Western-style toilets are standard in apartments and hotels.

➜ It is handy to remember the characters for men (男; *nán*) and women (女; *nǚ*).

➜ Many places ask you not to flush toilet paper but to put it in the waste-paper basket beside the toilet.

Dos & Don'ts

➜ **Transport** Be aware of priority seating in buses and the MRT (the seat is usually a different colour). Most Taiwanese would never think of sitting here

unless they are disabled, aged or pregnant. They also readily give up their seat to anyone who needs it.

➜ **Queues** Taiwanese queue for transport and in shops.

➜ **Shopping** Bargaining is not common. Handing over cash with two hands, a smile and a thank you (*xièxiè*) will go down well.

Tourist Information

➜ **Welcome to Taiwan** (eng.taiwan.net.tw) is the official site of the Taiwan Tourism Bureau.

➜ There are 10 Taipei Visitor Information Centres across the city, providing maps and pamphlets, and staffed with English-speaking friendly workers. The most useful ones are in Taipei 101 MRT (9am-9pm), Ximen MRT (9am-9pm) and Taipei Main Station in the Breeze Centre (8am-8pm)

➜ The **Tourist Hotline** (📞0800-011 765) is a really useful 24-hour service in English, Japanese and Chinese.

Travellers with Disabilities

➜ Seating and parking places for people with

disabilities are respected, but in general Taipei is not a very accessible environment. Street footpaths are uneven, kerbs are steep, and public transport, other than the MRT and HSR, is not equipped with wheelchair access.

➜ **Taiwan Access for All Association** (https://twaccess4all.wordpress.com) provides advice and assistance for travellers with disabilities.

➜ Download Lonely Planet's free Accessible Travel guide from http://lptravel.to/Accessible Travel

Visas

➜ Tourists from most European countries, Canada, the US, Australia (until December 2017; see Taiwan's Ministry of Foreign Affairs website for updates), New Zealand, South Korea and Japan are given visa-free entry for stays of up to 90 days.

➜ For visa extensions or any immigration enquiries, head to the **National Immigration Agency** (15 Guangzhou St, Ⓜ Xiaonanmen).

Language

The official language of Taiwan is referred to in the west as Mandarin Chinese. The Chinese call it Pǔtōnghuà (common speech) and in Taiwan it is known as Guóyǔ (the national language). Taiwanese, often called a 'dialect' of Mandarin, is in fact a separate language and the two are not mutually intelligible.

Mandarin has 'tonal' quality – the raising and lowering of pitch on certain syllables. There are four tones in Mandarin, plus a fifth 'neutral' tone that you can all but ignore. In Pinyin the tones are indicated with accent marks on vowels: ā (high), á (rising), ǎ (falling-rising), à (falling).

To enhance your trip with a phrasebook, visit **lonelyplanet.com**.

Basics

Hello.	您好.	Nín hǎo.
Goodbye.	再見.	Zàijiàn.
Yes.	是.	Shì.
No.	不是.	Bùshì.
Please.	請.	Qǐng.
Thank you.	謝謝.	Xièxie.
You're welcome.	不客氣.	Bùkèqì.
Excuse me.	請問	Qǐng wèn.

What's your name?

請問您貴姓?   Qǐngwèn nín guìxìng?

My name is ...

我姓 . . .   Wǒ xìng ...

Do you speak English?

你會講英文嗎?   Nǐ huì jiǎng yīngwén ma?

I don't understand.

我聽不懂.   Wǒ tīngbùdǒng.

Eating & Drinking

I'm vegetarian.

我吃素.   Wǒ chī sù.

I don't want MSG.

我不要味精.   Wǒ bú yào wèijīng.

Not too spicy.

不要太辣.   Bú yào tài là.

Let's eat.

吃飯.   Chī fàn.

Cheers!

乾杯!   Gānbēi!

Shopping

I'd like to buy ...

我想買 . . .   Wǒ xiǎng mǎi ...

I'm just looking.

我只是看看.   Wǒ zhǐshì kànkan.

How much is it?

多少錢?   Duōshǎo qián?

That's too expensive.

太貴了.   Tài guìle.

Is there anything cheaper?

有便宜一點的嗎?   Yǒu piányí yīdiǎn de ma?

Emergencies

Help!	救命啊!	Jiùmìng a!
Go away!	別煩我!	Bié fán wǒ!

Call a doctor!

請叫醫生！　　　　　Qǐng jiào yīshēng!

Call the police!

請叫警察！　　　　　Qǐng jiào jǐngchá!

I'm lost.

我迷路了．　　　　　Wǒ mílùle.

I'm ill.

我生病了．　　　　　Wǒ shēngbìngle.

Time & Numbers

What's the time?

幾點？　　　　　　　Jǐ diǎn?

... hour　　　　　... 點　　　... diǎn

... minute　　　　... 分　　　... fēn

in the morning

早上　　　　　　　　zǎoshàng

in the afternoon

下午　　　　　　　　xiàwǔ

in the evening

晚上　　　　　　　　wǎnshàng

yesterday　　　昨天　　　zuótiān

today　　　　　今天　　　jīntiān

tomorrow　　　明天　　　míngtiān

1	一	yī
2	二/兩	èr/liǎng
3	三	sān
4	四	sì
5	五	wǔ
6	六	liù
7	七	qī
8	八	bā
9	九	jiǔ
10	十	shí

Transport & Directions

Where is (the) ...?

... 在哪裡？　　　　... zài nǎlǐ?

What is the address?

地址在哪裡？　　　　Dìzhǐ zài nǎlǐ?

Could you write the address, please?

能不能請你把　　　　Néngbùnéng qǐng nǐ bǎ

地址寫下來？　　　　dìzhǐ xiě xiàlái?

I want to go to ...

我要去 ...　　　　　Wǒ yào qù ...

Can you show me on the map?

你能不能　　　　　　Nǐ néng bùnéng

(在地圖上)　　　　　(zài dìtú shàng)

指給我看？　　　　　zhǐ gěi wǒ kàn?

Go straight ahead.

一直走．　　　　　　Yīzhí zǒu.

at the next corner

在下一個轉角　　　　zài xià yīge zhuǎnjiǎo

at the traffic lights

在紅綠燈　　　　　　zài hónglùdēng

What time　　　... 幾點　　　... jǐdiǎn

does the ...　　開/到？　　　kāi/dào?

leave/arrive?

boat	船	chuán
city bus	公車	gōngchē
intercity bus	客運	kèyùn
minibus	小型公車	xiǎoxíng gōngchē
plane	飛機	fēijī
train	火車	huǒchē

I'd like a ... ticket.

我要一張...　　　　Wǒ yào yìzhāng...

票．　　　　　　　　.. piào.

one-way	單程	dānchéng
return	來回	láihuí

Behind the Scenes

Send Us Your Feedback

We love to hear from travellers – your comments help make our books better. We read every word, and we guarantee that your feedback goes straight to the authors. Visit **lonelyplanet.com/contact** to submit your updates and suggestions.

Note: We may edit, reproduce and incorporate your comments in Lonely Planet products such as guidebooks, websites and digital products, so let us know if you don't want your comments reproduced or your name acknowledged. For a copy of our privacy policy visit lonelyplanet.com/privacy.

Dinah's Thanks

I would like to thank all the friendly Taiwanese people who helped me along the way, especially Aidan Chuang, who truly has his finger on the pulse of Taipei's heartbeat. I am also grateful to my editor, Megan, for being so patient, and Miguel Fialho, who listened patiently day after day! Lastly I would like to thank Taiwan itself, a kind and generous host to all visitors.

Acknowledgements

Cover photograph: Xinyi District skyline, NH/Shutterstock ©

This Book

This first edition of Lonely Planet's *Pocket Taipei* guidebook was researched and written by Dinah Gardner. This guidebook was produced by the following:

Destination Editor Megan Eaves

Product Editors Joel Cotterell, Catherine Naghten

Senior Cartographer Julie Sheridan

Book Designers Michael Buick, Wendy Wright

Assisting Editors Imogen Bannister, Janice Bird, Andrea Dobbin, Victoria Harrison

Assisting Book Designers Clara Monitto, Jessica Rose

Cover Researcher Naomi Parker

Thanks to Carolyn Boicos, Cheree Broughton, Jennifer Carey, David Carroll, Neill Coen, Daniel Corbett, Jane Grisman, Corey Hutchison, Lauren Keith, Alison Lyall, Kate Mathews, Claire Naylor, Karyn Noble, Martine Power, Angela Tinson, Dora Whitaker

Index

See also separate subindexes for:

Eating p157
Drinking p157
Entertainment p158
Shopping p158

Sights 000
Map Pages **000**

Sights 000
Map Pages **000**

Sights **000**
Map Pages **000**

Our Writer

Dinah Gardner

Dinah is a freelance writer focusing on travel and politi
Since 2015 she has been happily based in Taiwan, one
of Asia's most charming and courteous countries. She
lived in and written about Vietnam, Tibet, China, Hong
Kong, Nepal and Bhutan.

Published by Lonely Planet Global Limited
CRN 554153
1st edition – May 2017
ISBN 978 1 78657 524 1
© Lonely Planet 2017   Photographs © as indicated 2017
10 9 8 7 6 5 4 3 2 1
Printed in Singapore